250

A Guideposts Book for Christian Living

COPING
Phyllis Hobe

Guideposts
Carmel, New York 10512

Dedicated to

Frank S. Mead, a disciple

ACKNOWLEDGMENTS

Excerpts from FAITH, HOPE AND LOVE by Charles L. Allen, copyright © 1982 by Fleming H. Revell Company. Published by Fleming H. Revell Company. Used by permission.

Excerpts from THE CHARLES L. ALLEN TREASURY by Charles L. Allen, copyright © 1970 by Fleming H. Revell Company. Published by Fleming H. Revell Company. Used by permission.

Excerpts from ANGER, DEFUSING THE BOMB by Ray Burwick. Published by Tyndale House Publishers, Inc., © 1981 by Ray Burwick. Used by permission.

Selections from LOVE by Leo F. Buscaglia, Ph.D., Charles B. Slack, Inc., 1972.

Excerpts from HOW TO DEAL WITH DIFFICULT PEOPLE by Andrew Costello, copyright © 1980, Liguori Publications, One Liguori Drive, Liguori, Missouri, 63057. Used with permission of copyright owner. All rights reserved.

Excerpts from EMOTIONS—CAN YOU TRUST THEM? by Dr. James Dobson. Copyright © 1980, Regal Books, Ventura, CA, 93006. Used by permission.

Excerpts from WHAT WIVES WISH THEIR HUSBANDS KNEW ABOUT WOMEN by Dr. James Dobson. Published by Tyndale House Publishers, Inc., © 1975. Used by permission.

Excerpts from GET RID OF ANXIETY AND STRESS by Toby Rice Drews. Copyright © 1982 by Toby Rice Drews. Reprinted by permission of Bridge Publishing, Inc., S. Plainfield, New Jersey, 07080.

Excerpts from GETTING THEM SOBER by Toby Rice Drews. Copyright © 1980 by Toby Rice Drews. Reprinted by permission of Bridge Publishing, Inc., S. Plainfield, New Jersey, 07080.

Excerpt from GIVE US THIS DAY OUR DAILY BREAD by Colleen Townsend Evans. Copyright © 1981 by Colleen Townsend Evans and Laura Hobe. Reprinted by permission of Doubleday & Company, Inc.

TABLE OF CONTENTS

INTRODUCTION
The Keys to Abundant Living

When I was a child, I spent much of my time with my great-grand-mother. Her name was Mary, and I called her Gram-ma for short. So did everyone else in our family.

Before I was old enough to attend school, my mother used to drop me off at Gram-ma's house early each weekday morning on her way to work. Then she would pick me up after five. When I went to school, I walked to Gram-ma's house each afternoon and waited there for my mother to come and get me.

Gram-ma was a tiny woman with heavy white hair wound into a thick knot at the back of her head. Her eyes were clear blue and serious. Although it was said she could speak seven languages fluently, I never heard her speak anything but English. Her voice was soft and very often I could see her lips moving as she went about the house making it shine, but I couldn't always hear the words. When I was close enough to hear, it seemed to me she was speaking to someone I couldn't see. Years later, I listened more carefully and found out Gram-ma was praying. She had a running conversation with God in which she discussed everything, from the huge tubs of laundry she still did by hand for her widowed son and his two daughters who lived nearby, to the state of world affairs, about which she was extremely well informed. Gram-ma and God were good friends.

Everything about my Gram-ma was good. She was a loving mother and grandparent, strict in her principles, unmovable in her adherence to what she believed was right, yet quick to forgive and embrace the forgiven. You

1

could talk to her about anything and know you had her complete attention and concern. She was a firm and compassionate nurse, so there was almost always a family member recuperating in one of Gram-ma's spare bedrooms —and loving every minute of it. If you needed encouragement, you could get it from Gram-ma. If you were weak in purpose—shilly-shallying, she called it—she'd tell you that, too, and before you knew it you'd be back on course. She'd lend you money if you really needed it, and not too much, but you had to pay it back, every penny of it. And she always had something baking in that big, old iron stove of hers that everybody told her was out of style and ought to be replaced. I still love the smell of gingerbread because to me it means Gram-ma.

Her life wasn't easy, now that I think about it. She was the only girl among several boys and she had to fight her whole family to get the education that meant so much to her. She taught school for a while until the pressure to get married became too much for her. Then she gave in—but, curiously, only after she met tall, gaunt-cheeked Joseph Moore, the man who would become my great-grandfather. And even though Gram-ma got off to a late start in marriage, she had seven children in quick succession, all of them tall like their father, and towering over their diminutive mother. Size didn't intimidate Gram-ma. One word from her, sometimes only a certain glance would do, and it was "Yes, ma'am," and hat in hand from even the most rambunctious son. They were good kids, and Gram-ma kept them clean, well-fed and sturdily dressed, all with her own two hands. She also taught them how to read and write before they went to school, and the first thing they did when they came home each day was sit down at the dining room table and do their homework. *Then* they could go out to play.

It was said that Gram-ma and my great-grandfather were extremely close, closer than most couples were in those days. And that was a blessing, because their time together was short. My great-grandfather fell ill in his late thirties and spent the next ten years in a wheel chair. In the last year of his life, I'm told, he would sit in front of the kitchen window, his head tilted to one side, and murmur one word over and over every time he took a breath: *Mary*.

My grandmother's family had a small lumber business and Gram-ma began working in the office part-time after her husband died. It helped her make ends meet. Somehow she still managed to keep her house and her children spotless, and she was always home when it mattered. She had a way of knowing when one of her children needed to talk.

Like most families, some of the children did well and some didn't. But somehow all their problems ended up at Gram-ma's. Even her sisters and brothers turned to her for help with their children, and sometimes there were cousins living in her house for a year or two while they got straightened out. Gram-ma just never gave up on them, and eventually they proved her to be right.

You see, Gram-ma was a Christian—in the most natural, uncomplicated way one can be a Christian. She simply loved her Lord and never made a move without Him. People who didn't spend as much time with her as I did used to think her constant whispered conversation was a sign of old age. They didn't have the opportunity, as I did, to find out what she was saying and to Whom. But Gram-ma never worried about what anyone thought, not even anyone in her own family. She paid more attention to what God thought, because that was important.

My great-grandmother was a character, no doubt about it. A genuine character, and I adored not only the woman but her uniqueness. One of the special treats in my young life was to see Gram-ma sit down in the big, rust-colored plush chair in the parlor and reach for the large black leather Bible on the table next to the chair. She would place the book on her lap, open its tissue-thin pages and look over in my direction, a childlike eagerness in her blue eyes. That was the only signal I needed and I was across the room like a shot from a bow. Squeezing myself into the chair next to her I would follow her finger as it traced the beloved words on the pages before us.

Gram-ma read beautifully. She gave meaning and interpretation to every word. Very often she would stop and describe exactly what was happening in words that were easier for me to understand. She knew the geographical setting for every biblical event. She knew what men and women were wearing right down to the texture of the cloth. She always made me feel she was introducing me to her close friends, and I was thrilled to be allowed to spend time in such company.

That was Gram-ma. I loved her very much and wanted more than anything to be just like her when I grew up. I wanted to be a good person. It seemed to me like the happiest thing in the world.

I was fifteen when Gram-ma suffered a stroke and I remember sitting on a metal chair at the foot of her hospital bed, unable to comprehend that this woman was going to die. She was in her eighties, but she had always been so strong in body and spirit that she never seemed old to any of us who were gathered there to say good-bye. None of us ever thought Gram-ma would die. And therefore we would not die. She was our strength. What would we do without her? How could God do this to us? And to her? She lay so still under the bed linens. Only her eyes could move, the rest of her was paralyzed. Was this her reward for being a good person? Didn't it make any difference in her life that she was a Christian? How could she even talk to her Lord now that her lips couldn't move?

Outside the hospital window the sun was rising over the city rooftops and the day was going to be beautiful. But it had no effect on me. It was too far away, and I couldn't help thinking that my Christian faith was like that sunrise—lovely, but outside the room where my life was taking place. My great-grandmother's long white hair was loose and lying spread about the pillow. I had never seen it that way before and it disturbed me. She seemed so helpless with her hair untethered.

Yet Gram-ma's eyes reached out to each one of us in that room and I had the feeling she was trying to speak to us, urgently, silently. The others sensed it, too, and kept asking her if there was something we could do to make her comfortable. Did she want her lips moistened? Her pillow turned? Her temples rubbed? Blink your eyes, Gram-ma, if you mean Yes. But she didn't blink, not deliberately, and we weren't able to interpret what it was she wanted to say before she died. But she did die, and in a surprisingly peaceful moment. I thought I even saw a smile in her eyes just before she closed them.

I wasn't so sure after that that I wanted to grow up to be like Gram-ma. I wasn't sure I wanted to give so much of myself to life and get so little in return. I remember one of Gram-ma's favorite Bible verses:

"I am come that they might have life, and that they might have it more abundantly"

(John 10:10, KJV)

The Living Bible translates it:

"My purpose is to give life in all its fullness."

Did Gram-ma really have abundance? Did she receive anywhere near as much as she gave? I wondered about that. It seemed to me there ought to be some kind of a reward for being a good person. And for being a Christian. If there was, then Gram-ma missed out on it, as far as I could see.

I was experiencing what Wayne Oates described some years later (*Your Particular Grief*):

. . .You may have had smooth sailing thus far. Your strenuous efforts to cope with life have been regularly rewarded with success. You have come to expect not reversal but achievement. Now this! What a rude awakening! Now you can no longer assume everything is going to go your way.

Spiritually, I was sulking. I was pulling back from life and keeping to its fringes for fear of getting hurt. Many of us do that and I can understand why. We can't see the sense in giving without getting. Goodness is not its own reward. We want more than that. Life *has* to be more than that. If not, why did God create it? I didn't think I would find an answer to that question, and if I did, I might not like it. Better to play it safe, I decided. Better not to risk so much by giving. I didn't want to end up disappointed. Like Gram-ma.

But was she disappointed? That wasn't what I saw in her eyes the last day of her life. It was something quite different. And I kept seeing it in the eyes of some other people.

I'm thinking of the man who taught me most of what I ever learned about writing. He wrote some of the best books I have ever read, but he didn't make a lot of money out of them. He might have if he had written more. But he spent too much time teaching others how to "build your words on the truth" and how to "make a sentence move." "I'll get around to it," he used to say when I begged him to put more of his thoughts on paper. And sometimes he did. But more often he never had the time. He gave most of it to others. Yet there was that same expression in his eyes—that happiness Gram-ma had in hers.

And the couple I used to see walking their little girl along our street—until one day I didn't see them for a long time. Then, when I did, I learned that the little girl had died. How terrible! How unexpected! Yes, it was terrible. But not unexpected. A week after the child was born the parents were told she wouldn't live more than a few years. So the parents decided those years would be the most enjoyable, loving, normal years they could provide. It wasn't easy for them to allow themselves to love like that—as if nothing was going to end it—but they did it. And there was that same expression in their eyes. That happiness. As Ann Weems reminds us:

> But life is more than birthday parties;
> Life is more than candied apples.

I saw that look again when I talked to Ken, the carpenter who used to come by my parents' house in the late afternoons to screen in their back porch. Ken taught shop in a school for troubled boys, so he could only work as a carpenter for a few hours each day. He had his own business once, my parents told me, but one of his customers moved out of town without paying for a large addition to a house, and Ken had to find another way to make a living. He owed his suppliers a lot of money for the materials they had furnished him, but he paid them back in full. It took years, but he never complained. There were ways he could have avoided going into debt, but he wasn't comfortable with them. He didn't want to put anyone else out of business.

"Do you ever think of starting your own business again?" I asked him once.

"Sure," he said. "Every now and then. But I like what I'm doing now. I like these kids. And maybe I can get to them before they turn out like the man who skipped town on me."

There it was again—that something Gram-ma had. Was it—could it possibly have been—*life in all its fullness*? Was I wrong about the giving and getting? Do we get by giving?

Perhaps.

Being a Christian is not for cowards. God's fellowship is liable to lead a person into "such terribly exciting truth that the stubborn human littleness in us shies off at the merest mention of Him" (John Hercus, *More Pages From God's Casebook*). Fear says it's best to stay on the safe side, giving a slight nod to Him now and again, in case we ever need His power to bail us out of an extreme distress—like a desperately ill child or an unfaithful husband. The trouble is that God remains a stranger, so unknown that you can begin to wonder if He is even real.

Gladys Hunt

Perhaps that was what I had yet to learn from Christ's own experience here among us.

. . . For when I take hold of him I take hold of the very self of God. This Word is not a spelled out Word, it is a lived-out Word.

E. Stanley Jones

He was in the thick of life, never on its fringes. He was a devoted son and family member, a careful craftsman, a loyal friend, an honorable citizen in a corrupt society. He was the Son of God, come to save the soul of man, yet He took time to stop along the road and touch the eyes of a blind man,

7

restoring his sight. Thirsty and tired, He listened caringly to a woman beside a well and changed the way she would live the rest of her days. He made a wedding party festive by His presence. He yielded to the tug of an ailing woman at His sleeve when the crowd surely pressed too closely around Him. He could love the undiscovered strength in a frightened friend. He could kiss His betrayer. He could withhold the destruction He might have brought down upon His persecutors. Agonizing on the cross, He beheld the sorrow of His mother and provided for her comforting. Dying, He gave life to all who would believe in this miracle of love.

Was that life in all its fullness? Was that abundance? Oh, yes. At last I was beginning to understand.

It had something to do with the way Gram-ma used to talk to God all the time. She knew Him as I wanted to know Him, but never had. And she knew Him through living her life as a Christian.

We are not here to give and to get and to be good persons, vital as all those qualities are. We are here to do the Lord's work, to live as He lived when He was among us. We are here to give something to life, not to get something back from it. This I have learned not only from Christ's own example, but from others who have that same look of happiness in their eyes when I know very well that their experiences are not always happy as I would define the word. I learned it from the wonderful senior gentleman who was my teacher in more than the art of writing. From the couple who walked with their child in joy even though they knew it would not last. From Ken, who was too concerned to be bitter. And from many other Christians who have shared their abundant lives with me through their words, spoken and written.

Being a Christian is not an easy way to live. It isn't smiling all the time or bearing up under great burdens without complaint. It isn't making do or savoring one triumph after another. Being a Christian means calling on God to help you cope with life. It's my great-grandmother making a difference in this world by meeting problems head-on or finding a way to live with them. It's what you do with dreams that *don't* come true as well as those that do. It's being dead serious about learning what Jesus Christ would do— and can do—in your situation. It's understanding what it means, and what it takes, to become His disciple—today. It's giving out of your own need. It's living in the real world, as a real person, with a real Saviour. You won't be spared anything, but a lot more will be asked of you.

Believing in Christ is not enough to make us His disciples. We have to be willing to live the way He does. We have to find the answer to the question, "What would He do in my situation?" and then do it. That is how a Christian copes.

And now I would like to share something with you. It is something most personal: my faith. For I know now that being a Christian does make a difference in our lives. Not that we receive any reward for our faith. If anything, we are challenged to do more, to be more, and to discover who we are. For we are more than you and I as persons, more than men and women, or citizens. We are children of God. We are far more than physical beings. We are spiritual persons, with spiritual features as plain as the nose on your face.

There is, in each Christian, a portion of God our Father. We resemble Him because we have inherited many of His magnificent qualities. But on our own we may have difficulty recognizing them or even realizing that they are ours. We are like the ordinary people Jesus called to follow Him. We need Him to show us, to teach us, who we are and what we can do. And we need to learn from Him every day through coping with life's situations. Christ is our mirror. He reflects what and who we are and how we are to meet each day.

For we are meant to be in the thick of life, just as He was. We are meant to feel the whole range of human emotions, just as He did. We are created to laugh as well as weep, to be lonely as well as rejoicing in fellowship. We can hope and be disappointed, and yet hope again. We can be totally exhausted, and yet give to another in need of strength. We can feel anger at injustice, and pray for the unjust. We can hate sin, and forgive the sinner. We can be ministered to in our need, and then share that blessing with another. And yet another. There is no end. There never is a time when we are completely Christian, or when we are finished growing more like Christ.

I wish I could go back and sit at the foot of Gram-ma's hospital bed again, because I think I know now what she was trying to tell all of us with her eyes. I think she wanted us to know that she was not defeated or helpless.

That she could indeed talk to her Lord, whether or not her lips could move, because truly she spoke to Him with her whole life. Her physical existence was ending, she knew that better than we did, but she was not at all disappointed. Her life would go on, but the earthly span had been good. She had lived it as a disciple, coping with every moment as Christ would have done. And her life, like His, had been abundant.

I would like my life to be as full.

In these pages you will read the words of many men and women who have coped with life's sorrows, joys, problems and challenges as Christians. As God's children, endowed with spiritual resources and strengths. As contemporary disciples of Jesus Christ—who met our same predicaments, knew our cares and anxieties. They will tell you how abundant the life of discipleship can be.

May their discoveries help you, as they have helped me, to appreciate all of life as truly a gift from God. And to grow every day closer to Him.

Phyllis Hobe

PART I

BECOMING A DISCIPLE

1

YOU DON'T HAVE TO BE PERFECT

Being a Christian means that you do not go through life alone. Even in your most solitary moments, God is at your side in the person of His Son and in the presence of His Spirit. You walk with God's hand in yours.

Be assured, you will not always walk on level ground and the way will not always be smooth. You will climb steep hills, cling to the side of inhospitable mountains, stumble into holes you can't see in the dark; you will know severe cold and unkind heat, rain and snow will drench and chill you. You will not always be filled by what you eat nor will you always be pleased with your shelter. Sometimes you may need to take refuge from all that you know; you may need to seek an alien land. Your friends will not always be your friends; some of them will desert you, some may turn against you.

And you will be blessed with the fullest, most meaningful life there is—because being a Christian means letting Christ influence everything you do. It means allowing His personality, His way of thinking, His strength and His tenderness to affect your whole person and all your decisions, relationships, actions and inner life. You don't have to be perfect; you just have to be His.

But don't be afraid to go where He leads you. Don't pull back when you see difficulties ahead. Let Him guide you through them. Let Him hold you up when you are weary. You may get hurt, but He will heal you. If you are anxious, He'll understand and He will tell you about the times when He, too, trembled. Your weakness is not your shame. You are human, and so is He.

But He is also divine, and He will share with you the spiritual resources His Father gave to Him. They will bring meaning and purpose to your earthly life—as they did to His.

So let Him take your hand. Let Him teach you the kind of trust, love and obedience that made His life unique. You are God's partner in this world. You are meant to do more than experience this life. You can grow through your experience; you can be strengthened by your struggles. Your own feelings can make you more sensitive to the feelings of others. As you discover your own worth as a human being, your cup will run over and you will pour out of it into the cup of another. This is the way a Christian lives.

2

GIVING UP OUR GOLDEN CALVES

There was a time when I had little sympathy for the Israelites. I didn't understand how they could emerge from the wilderness, delivered by God Himself, and then make a calf out of gold and bow down to it. How could anyone prefer an idol to the Living God? I never would have done such a thing.

It took years for me to realize that I did "such a thing" repeatedly. Yes, I had other gods, and they came between me and my Lord as surely as any golden calf I might have cast with my own hands.

My other gods were quite respectable, which is why I was so long in identifying them. Some of them seemed to be gifts from God Himself.

For instance, I have always wanted to be a good person, and I put a lot of effort into that striving. I gave thought to what I did and said to others. I weighed the advantages and disadvantages of aiding causes. I tried to consult my conscience often. I thought I knew what was right and decent in this world, and I meant to move in that direction.

Righteousness—that was one of my other gods.

I tried to be a devoted daughter to my mother, who is still living, and to my stepfather, who, with patience and a steadfast concern, replaced the father I had lost. I wanted to become the person they wanted me to be, yet I didn't always succeed.

Duty—another god.

I fell in love, more than once, and finally committed my future to a partnership with someone I worshiped as much as any person can worship another. We had wonderful plans for our future—children, a home, achievements, growing old together, becoming part of an ongoing creation.

Adoration—another god.

I loved my work from the first moment my child-sized fingers clenched a stubby pencil and pushed it across a paper, intending to print letters of the alphabet and drawing instead wiggly lines which no one, not even I, could decipher. I vowed from that early time that I would be a writer, that somehow I would find a way to put my thoughts and feelings into readable words.

Determination—another god.

I also wanted to be successful and be recognized for doing good work. I wanted to reach a point in my life where I didn't have to try so hard to be accepted for what I am.

Ambition—another god.

I have always appreciated the essence of life. I could find it in the barest tree in winter, and in spring I was constantly in celebration. God's world was sacred to me.

Custodianship—another god.

Friends—life's greatest treasures! Some old, some new, some forever and some just passing by. As long as I had a friend in this world, I was not alone.

Cherishing—like the rest, another god.

Then there was my faith in God and in Jesus Christ, His Son. That went without saying. I wanted to be a good Christian. I wanted to speak the truth, to deal honestly with everyone I knew, and to live in the spirit of brotherly love.

Piety—assuredly, another god.

All these were my golden calves, and you should know about them. I did not for a moment want to give them up—yet now I realize that they made it impossible for me to live as a Christian.

> Thou shalt have no other gods before me...
> *(Exodus 20:3, KJV)*

Whenever we put anyone, anything, any goal, desire or value between ourselves and our God, then we are bowing down to a golden calf.

> Thou shalt not make unto thee any graven image, or any likeness of any thing that is in heaven above, or that is in the earth beneath, or that is in the water under the earth. Thou shalt not bow down thyself to them, nor serve them: for I the Lord thy God am a jealous God...
> *(Exodus 20:4–5, KJV)*

God does not want to isolate me or impoverish me. He is not putting me to the test, telling me I must give up the people, the values, the goals and aspirations that are important to me. I can love my parents and my friends. I can do everything in my power to make my family happy. I can try to be a good person and hope to gain recognition for worthy work. I can proclaim my faith. I can do all those things whether or not I am a Christian.

But I must not—*ever*—put those things first in my life. Important as they are, God must come before them. If I should ever have to choose one from among them all, then the choice must be: God.

Nor can I allow myself to be created in the image, or in the expectations, of those who love me. Only God can create, and recreate, me.

> . . .The Christian is in a different position from other people who are trying to be good. They hope, by being good, to please God if there is one, or—if they think there is not—at least they hope to deserve approval from good men. But the Christian thinks any good he does comes from the Christ-life inside him. He does not think God will love us because we are good, but that God will make us good because He loves us, just as the roof of a greenhouse does not attract the sun because it is bright, but becomes bright because the sun shines on it.
>
> *C. S. Lewis*

I cannot be the person my parents want me to be. They may believe that what they want is the best for me, but only God *knows* what I must do and be and become.

> Jesus stayed behind in Jerusalem. His parents didn't miss him the first day, for they assumed he was with friends among the other travelers. But when he didn't show up that evening, they started to look for him. . . .Three days later they finally discovered him. He was in the Temple, sitting among the teachers of Law, discussing deep questions with them and amazing everyone with his understanding and answers.
>
> His parents didn't know what to think. "Son!" his mother said to him. "Why have you done this to us? Your father and I have been frantic, searching for you everywhere."
>
> "But why did you need to search?" he asked. "Didn't you realize that I would be here at the Temple, in my Father's House?" But they didn't understand what he meant.
>
> *(Luke 2:43–50, Living Bible)*

I cannot live up to the expectations of my friends, encouraging as they may be. My friends may not approve of the path God wants me to walk.

> From that time forth began Jesus to shew unto his disciples, how that he must go unto Jerusalem, and suffer many things of the elders and chief priests and scribes, and be killed, and be raised again the third day.
> Then Peter took him and began to rebuke him, saying, Be it far from thee, Lord: this shall not be unto thee.
> But he turned, and said unto Peter, Get thee behind me, Satan: thou art an offence unto me: for thou savourest not the things that be of God, but those that be of men.
>
> *(Matthew 16:21–23, KJV)*

My family cannot claim all there is of me, much as I might want to give myself to them. I do not belong to them—or to anyone. I belong to God.

> For I am come to set a man at variance against his father, and the daughter against her mother, and the daughter-in-law against her mother-in-law.
> And a man's foes shall be they of his own household.
> He that loveth father or mother more than me is not worthy of me: and he that loveth son or daughter more than me is not worthy of me.
>
> *(Matthew 10:35–37, KJV)*

And my work? I cannot allow my work to persuade me I am a Christian simply because I am using my talents in God's behalf. They are His talents, not mine, and He is the only one Who can direct me how to use them.

Instead of preaching the good news of the Kingdom, He was forced to saw planks and hammer nails. It was such menial work for the Son of God to be doing. It caused Him to miss going to college. Every day He held back, it seemed, was a day lost. But the days went into months and into years, and still He had to wait. His chance did not come until He was thirty years old. In those days, thirty years old was approaching old age.

But as you study His entire life, you begin to feel that the waiting was part of God's plan. Certainly Jesus used His circumstances in the finest possible way. Instead of becoming bitter, instead of surrendering His dreams, instead of turning to some lesser purpose, He held fast to His promised land and at the same time was faithful to life, day by day. As we study His later ministry, we see that the opportunities of His limited "today" became the stones out of which He built His castle tomorrow.

Charles L. Allen

I must point out that no one ever asked to be one of my other gods. No goal or prize or status or emotional fulfillment was that important, either. *I* set my loved ones up on pedestals. *I* cast my needs and wishes into golden calves. The craftsmanship was mine alone. *I* freely gave them what belonged to God—absolute dominion over my life.

So when I tried to follow Christ, I was like the Rich Young Ruler with a fortune in golden statuettes, being told to go and sell them all. It seemed too great a price to pay. After all, hadn't I lived by God's rules? Wasn't that enough? I had obeyed the commandments handed down by God Himself.

Except for one. . . .

Like the Rich Young Ruler, I had forgotten the first commandment, the one about "no other gods." In my haste to get on to the easier stipulations, I had skipped that one. I assumed that my other good deeds were proof of my faith—and so they may be. But that first commandment *is* my faith: Do I—or do I not—bow down to other gods?

I did, and I didn't know how to give them up. I too was about to "turn away sadly" when something terrible, yet wonderful, happened: Some of my other gods gave me up. They turned their faces away.

20

It began with a friend and a misunderstanding. We were in business together and we disagreed on how to proceed on an important project. So we went our separate ways. That's when the friendship ended.

Then my mother became seriously ill. Her leg had to be amputated, and in her agony she blamed everyone, including me, for her suffering. She withdrew from life and from all who tried to comfort her.

My father-in-law died suddenly, and my husband's grief was long and severe. I felt inadequate because no amount of my adoration could restore him.

Even my work brought no comfort. I sat down to blank page after blank page, and at the end of the day I tore up everything I had written on them. That had never happened to me before.

So there they were, all my other gods, and they couldn't help me. Even those who didn't turn away couldn't heal me. But standing alone in the emptiness of my life was the One True and Living God. He had not turned His face away. He never would.

> ...God allows us to have disappointments, frustrations, or even worse because He wants us to see that our joy is not in such wordly pleasures as success or money or popularity or health or sex or even in a miracle-working faith; our joy is in the fact that we have a relationship with God. Few of us ever understand that message until circumstances have divested us of any possibility of help except by God himself.
>
> *Catherine Marshall*

I expected some kind of reproof, but there was none. I was a welcome Prodigal, held close in loving arms. Could this be a "jealous" God?

In the Living Bible translation of Exodus 20:5, the word *possessive* is used in place of *jealous*. To our modern minds, possessive may not seem to be much of an improvement, because it has unpleasant connotations. We do not want to be possessed. We prize our freedom. How dare anyone—even God—put limitations on our lives? How dare anyone—even God—tell us what we can and cannot do?

I did not understand that to be possessed by the One True and Living God is the ultimate freedom. I was defining the word in human terms, remembering how my golden calves had limited me. I had not yet learned that the language of the Lord is different.

When God possesses us, He fashions us for freedom. He leads us into a discovery of who we are and shows us how to use the abilities He created in us. He does this by teaching us how a child of God is to live in this world. Our model is His Son.

Make no mistake about it, Jesus also had His struggles with other gods, the same ones you and I have. His parents, His friends, even His enemy, Pilate, urged Him to avoid conflict. Some of those who were close to Him were embarrassed by His miracles. He was, in the eyes of many, a local eccentric who was going to get into serious trouble if He didn't listen to reason. Instead, He listened to the voice of God, although sometimes it was hard for Him to hear it over the din of advice urging Him to go in another direction, become another kind of person, march to the beat of a thousand different drums, each one sounding out a different cadence.

But He listened. And He heard. Most important, when He heard the call of a golden calf, He reminded Himself that there is only One True and Living God. He would not bow down to a human counterfeit.

> . . .Christ never meant that we were to remain children in *intelligence*: on the contrary, He told us to be not only "as harmless as doves," but also "as wise as serpents." He wants a child's heart, but a grown-up's head. He wants us to be simple, single-minded, affectionate, and teachable, as good children are; but He also wants every bit of intelligence we have to be alert at its job, and in first class fighting trim.
>
> *C. S. Lewis*

You and I can still hear those same drumbeats. Some of them come from our own feelings—our pride, our allegiances, sympathies, angers and indignations. There are matters we want to correct in our world and we may think we know how to do it. There are loved ones who need us. Can we answer these calls without ending up at the feet of a golden calf?

We can—if we take God's hand instead of going our way alone.

We can—if we allow God, not other gods, to shape us into the persons He needs in His world.

We can—if we turn all our energies, our desires, our ambitions, our concerns and our love over to God and let Him put them to work in ways that will get results.

All of my life I had been influenced too much by the moods of my associates. When they were excited and panicked, I reflected their anxiety. Now. . .although I was still performing in the same circles. . .I was occasionally finding a calmness and an ability to live with more honesty and integrity than before. I was starting to play my life to a different audience—to the Living Christ. . . .I began to get up in the morning being conscious of God's awareness of me and my waking movements. I began being able to tell Him that He was the one for whom I wanted to perform the day's actions. Just the conscious act of deciding *that* was a new kind of commitment which, by itself, changed all kinds of things.

Keith Miller

When I took God's extended hand, I was a broken person, and I took a long time to be healed. But I *was* healed. There are scars and some signs of breakage, yet the healing is so strong that in many ways I am becoming a more effective person.

When I allowed myself to be shaped by my other gods, I was made up of bits and pieces intended to win favor at the feet of golden calves. No wonder I came apart under some of life's blows. And no wonder I didn't know who I was, because bits and pieces have no real identity.

Now I know who I am because I have been given my identity from God. I am the authentic child of my Heavenly Father. I am the person He created and there is no other like me. I am discovering my strengths and weaknesses as I walk through my life with His Son. And I will never break again. I can withstand any blows that may come. I can truly give of my growing self to those I love and find in need, and I can do it without fear of turning them into golden calves. Because, you see, there are no other gods. Not any more.

I am free now to be concerned about this world. I can comfort my suffering mother without altering the person God has intended me to be. I can cherish my friends without taking the paths they recommend for me. I can look after the well-being of my family and still maintain my own spiritual health. Instead of demonstrating my own goodness, I can become a channel for God's love and His inestimable goodness. Instead of pitting my fragile human energies against the obstacles in my way, I can call upon God's power to move them, go around them or climb over them, whichever He decides is best. This I can do through my trust in the One True and Living God.

3

THIS GREATER LOVE

We had been friends for years. I trusted her with my confidences and counted on her for advice that was intended for my well-being. I cared deeply about anything that concerned her. I felt pain from her slightest wound. I would begin cheering yards before she reached her desired goals. I cherished her family and her other friends. I was available in any time of need, at any moment of crisis, or even when the only requirement was silence and the full attention that a loving heart can give. And I was absolutely certain that my friend gave as much to me in return. I thought that was what friendship meant...a fair exchange.

Then, when I needed her most urgently, my friend let me down. I was in an accident and called on my friend to come to me. She said she would—and she didn't. I was not alone—please understand that—but I craved the presence of a special friend to help me get through the thousands of entanglements that follow an accident. My friend didn't refuse. On the contrary, she said she would be "right there." She never came. In fact, she behaved as if the accident never happened. But we both knew better. We knew the friendship was over.

The sad truth is, the friendship never really began. My friend and I never *really* loved each other—not, at least, in the way God loves. We loved in human ways, which is quite another matter. This word *love* means many things, depending on who is doing the loving.

Saying "Yes!" to God is not a simple matter because making our lives into lives of love is not a simple or easy thing. To choose love as a life principle means that my basic mind-set or question must be: What is the loving thing to be, to do, to say? My consistent response to each of life's events, to each person who enters and touches my life, to each demand on my time and nerves and heart, must somehow be transformed into an act of love. However, in the last analysis, it is this "Yes!" that opens me to God. Choosing love as a life principle widens the chalice of my soul, so that God can pour into me his gifts and graces and powers.

John Powell

A few months ago I brought a young puppy into our family. And our family includes a six-year-old cat, an exceptionally friendly and patient animal. The dog and cat started out agreeably. They boxed playfully and the cat submitted to the puppy's adoring licks. Then, as the puppy grew much larger than the cat, their playtime became somewhat perilous. The puppy, still adoring the cat, almost crushed him between her massive paws. The cat, defending his more fragile body, bit and clawed, at times dangerously close to the puppy's eyes. Still they tried to play because they loved each other, but it was evident to me that nature could not be left to take its course. It was going in the wrong direction. Someone, something, had to intervene.

I was the someone, and the something was a word—"gentle"—repeated firmly, not harshly, whenever the puppy and the cat played. When necessary I blocked the puppy's slamming paws and also caught a few of the cat's scratches on my hands. But the intervention worked. In time, two friendly animals began to respect each other's differences. Their capacity to love was not at all diminished, but rather, transformed. Nature's course was altered—for the better.

My friend and I were like the dog and cat, each of us trusting the other to be exactly what we assumed ourselves to be. Until something made us aware of our differences. We were not alike. We were not even what we imagined each other to be. In truth, we hardly knew each other. We loved what we thought we saw in each other, and we were afraid of differences. That's right, we loved in the way people do—naturally. After all, love is born in a person, isn't it?

No. It is not.

Love does *not* come naturally. It comes—or, rather, it grows—spiritually. It is born of God's intervention in human relationships. You and I might very well love each other to pieces. We might love each other to death. God would never do that. His love makes us whole. He loves us to life.

It turned out that my friend, the one who wouldn't come to me when I was injured, was not able to deal with my crisis, although I didn't realize it at that time. I didn't realize that she was afraid I was going to die, and she couldn't face that loss. Because I didn't know *her*, I didn't understand her fears. And *she* thought *I* was strong enough to face anything, even death, by myself. She didn't know *me*, or my frailties. All we knew, as we discovered the truth about each other, was that we weren't perfect. The friendship ended because we felt betrayed when we couldn't live up to each other's expectations. As "they" say, that's the way love goes.

Is it?

I wonder how comfortable I might be among the people Jesus called His friends. Would I like the loudmouthed Peter? And how might I react to him in the courtyard when Jesus was whipped and humiliated, and Peter denied even knowing the Man? Would that end my friendship with such a man, assuming we had one to begin with?

Good question.

And the Marys, any one of them? Could they be my friends? Mary, the mother, devoted as mothers are, but a bit too protective, fussy almost, too conscious of what other people might think, a don't-rock-the-boat type who, in today's world, might yearn to see her Son in a buttoned-down shirt and sitting behind a name plate at a plastic-chrome desk?

What about the other Mary, the one who washed Christ's feet with her tears? We all know her kind. She'll do anything to get a man's attention. Would I want to invite her to my home? For dinner? Would I even want it known we were acquainted?

I might be more attracted to the intellectual Mary, the sister of Martha. Yet I doubt very much that she was a person I could count on to come to my aid if my car broke down. She might have her nose buried in a book and forget I called for help.

I definitely would dislike Thomas. I don't get along with doubters. I prefer decisive people who take stands and know where they're going.

Don't even mention Paul. I admire the man. His strength and dedication humble me. But friends we could never be. We agree on things of the spirit, but not on the things of this world.

I could go on, and I'm sure I could find fault with everyone Jesus called friend. Our love for Christ might be the only thing we have in common. Aside from that, there are too many differences that would come between us. We would suffer too many disappointments.

I expect something from love. I am sorely disappointed when a friend can't sit up with me in a time of trial. I believe I would do as much *as* a friend. And if I knew someone I loved was going to deliver me to my enemies, I couldn't bring myself to share my last meal with him. I would hardly entrust my hopes, my purpose in life, to someone who let me down more than once.

But, then, I am not Christ. I do not love as He does.

I would ask myself how Jesus could choose such friends. I would weep over the agony they caused Him. I would marvel at His patience, and His ability to go on loving. He had all the world from which to choose His friends. God had all of time in which to send His Son to us; all of humanity from which to select His Son's earthly family. Why didn't God choose better?

Would it have mattered? Are any of us better?

> For the Son of man is come to seek and to save that which was lost.
>
> *(Luke 19:10, KJV)*

I, too, am one of the lost. So are you. If we think we love Jesus better, harder, more dependably than those who had the magnificent privilege of walking the dusty hot Jerusalem roads with Him, then we are wrong. I know I am. Consider this: I cannot continue to love the friend who didn't respond when I was hurt. I no longer keep in touch with a family member whose inner conflicts led her to alcoholism. I avoid the person whose lies caused me years of grief. When it comes to love, I am Zacchaeus, a tax collector in the pay of those who have conquered my sense of mercy, and I extract more than a fair dollar of bitterness for every grudge I bear.

No, I don't love as Christ does. I don't know how. And I am hiding high up in a tree of self-deception, telling myself that I will observe this Jesus from afar. I am afraid to meet Him face to face. He will introduce me to my sins, and I don't want to know them.

But He sees me. He calls me down from my leafy shelter and I cannot refuse His invitation. I climb down, and I am among the multitude. I am one of them, one of those He came to seek and to save. And in my humility there is hope.

What is this He wants me to give? I have no wealth.

Love, He tells me.

Love? I have loved all my life!

No, not truly.

I have loved as well as I can!

Not so.

I am only human.

No. More than that. I am His. He is mine. That makes a difference. I am more than myself.

God, the Eternal God, is Love. Covet therefore that everlasting gift, that one which it is certain is going to stand, that one coinage which will be current in the Universe when all other

29

coinages of all the nations of the world shall be useless and unhonoured. You will give yourself to many things, give yourself first to love.

Henry Drummond

When God decided to break into history with his own character, when he decided to share his love with the world, he decided to do it in personal, not ideological, terms. He came to us as Word in Flesh, Jesus Christ. Jesus Christ is the love of God breaking through and finding us where we really are. If we really want to know what love is, if we really want to get some kind of handle on the love of God, then we must consider Jesus Christ. We must look closely at him in the New Testament. We must watch him in action.

Earl F. Palmer

Now that I am among these friends of Jesus, I see that we are very much alike. I'm as fussy as His mother and quite concerned about how my faith "looks." Like Thomas, I find it hard to believe that the Son of God actually died for me—and would do it again without my asking. I keep thinking I'm going to wake up and discover it's all a dream. I am grateful for Christ's love, as Peter was, but in my heart I wish He would make it easier for me to love Him. I try to win His attention however I can, with the oils and ointments of my prayers, my thoughts and even my tears. I proclaim my devotion to Him, but when it comes to living by it, I am clumsy, totally at a loss.

Like the others, I do not love Him well. Yet I can't love anyone well until I learn how to love Him better. The human love I have offered all my life is not good enough, not for Him, for me or for those who matter to me. Its brittle surface breaks down under stress, exposing the touchy inner core. It grips too hard, insisting on something in return for what it gives. It runs dry, like the winding creek behind my house that bubbles and gurgles delightfully in times of heavy rain, yet turns into an ankle-twisting gully during the dry spells.

Even though we are made in His image, God often seems so different from us. Or, rather, we seem so different from Him. But with Christ's help we can at least begin to resemble Him. We have to begin with love. And our very first lesson is that we really don't know how to love at all. Oh, we think we know. We love all the time. We love everything and everyone. We. . .just. . .love.

Yet we don't. We only use the word. We mean well and we want to love. We have the capacity for it, given to us by God at the moment of our creation. But we follow human models. We love in the way others love and have loved since the beginning of the world. We keep making the same mistakes all over again. And so, like others before us, we find love to be a disappointing experience. Somehow, even at its human best, it never quite lives up to our expectations. Why is it, we wonder sadly, that love—always so blessed in the beginning—can turn on us, hurt us, consume us, distort who we are, resent what it once prized and even destroy us? What did we do wrong? Should we try again? Will another object of our love bring us better results?

Yes. Definitely.

The proper object of our love is God—Christ—the Holy Spirit. All three in one.

There is a better kind of love for us all. There is a kind of love that does not have to be initiated by something or someone wonderful. It simply exists. It expects nothing; it simply gives. It never controls; it negotiates. Instead of insisting that the person who is loved must meet the standards of the person who is loving, it honors the God-created differences between them. This is the way Jesus loves. He doesn't look at us and wish we could be better than we are. He sees our flaws. He doesn't excuse them, but He doesn't allow them to stop Him from loving the better parts of us. He forgives our imperfections, even when they wound Him, but He doesn't close His eyes to them. His is a "nevertheless" kind of love.

The miracle of grace that supports genuine friendship resides in the way people who wound each other are capable of healing each other, in the way people who fail each other can

31

also forgive each other. Friendship is not a smooth rink on which a marvelous and errorless brand of figure skating goes on without even scratching the surface. Friendship is a broken turf, full of the promise of spring, but also marred by the ditches and holes in which friends may stumble as they try to stick together.

Eugene Kennedy

I bask in this Jesus-love. Sitting close to the coals from the fire that cooked the meal He shared with us, I see my own happiness reflected in the glowing faces of the others. I am more than warmed by this love. It ministers to me in ways I didn't dream possible. Old wounds, roughly patched on the surface, are being healed thoroughly right down to where they used to throb so painfully. The weariness of disappointment is gone; the quick winds of hope sweep through me. I have energy, strength, purpose. I am flexible so that I can kneel to needs and yet stretch toward challenges. If I am knocked to the ground, I will get up again, over and over. If I am hurt, my cries will be heard and my pain shared, and I will be made whole again. I have meaning. I am loved.

I don't want to move from this place. Yet I must. He is telling me I must leave this warm firelight and go back into the world. But not up into the shelter of a high perch. I am to walk the earth, as He did, and encounter all manner of persons, events, situations. I am not to shrink from them. No, far from it. I am not the same as I was before. Neither is my love. I have within me a greater love, and it is not mine to keep. It is His love, and I must make use of it. It must influence each moment of my life.

But how?

In what specific ways?

What does this Jesus-love do?

It lets go. It does not possess the beloved.

God let His own Son go. Just as Jesus had misgivings about the reason for His coming, certainly His loving Father must have had second thoughts.

God loved His Son every bit as much as you and I love our children. The knowledge of Christ on the cross must have been an agony for His Father, and there must have been moments when God wondered if the torment was endurable. Or worthwhile. Here was a perfect young Man about to suffer all the penalties of the sins of far-from-perfect human beings who would sin again.

Could you, as a parent, let such a son go? Wouldn't you want to hold him back, keep him from pain and abuse? I know I would. Suddenly the reason for his sacrifice wouldn't be as compelling. As much as it might mean to those he was intended to save, their needs would seem very far away, while my son, at the moment of his sacrifice, would be as close as my own skin. Already I would begin to feel the puncture of the thorns, the spear in his side. And I don't know whether I could bear it.

But yes, I do know. The simple truth is that I wouldn't be able to go through with it. I would try to hold my son back, do anything I could to keep him from going, even if that were his wish.

We possessive persons are not evil. We are quite normally weak in wanting to hold onto those we love. But we are not evil. We mean well. We intend the best for those we love. Yet we do them the greatest amount of harm through that kind of loving.

We can offer help with a pure motive, but if the help isn't really needed, it isn't really helpful. On the other hand, sometimes we may offer help that is needed—but our motives may not be so pure. I'm sure we all can think of times when someone needed help and got it, but the giver then tried to manipulate the life of the receiver. . .We parents have to be particularly careful here.

"After all I've done for you, you're going to leave me?" Sound familiar?

I know of a father who has done countless so-called helpful things for his daughter, things that go far beyond the raising and educating of a child, things such as setting her up in business, providing her with a fine home, sending her on expensive trips. These may be the things most parents would love to do for their children if they were able, things that in themselves are beautiful if there are no strings attached. But they can be destructive if a parent does them as part of the after-all-I've-done-for-you game. And that's what this father has done. How sad it is to see a woman of forty who has never been free to pursue the dreams God has put in her heart because she suffers from a deep sense of guilt and a confused idea of what it means to honor her father.

Colleen Townsend Evans

I tell myself I am not God. Then I catch myself trying to play God in the lives of those I love. Of course, I fail. And, worst of all, I fail in my attempts to love.

One personality trait gets the prize for ruining more relationships than any other. It is a characteristic found to some degree in each of us, but when it gets out of hand, it is always destructive and always pushes people away.

I am talking about the tendency to control others. This villain frequently masquerades as love.

. . .We all require room to breathe. When promising relationships suddenly blow apart, it is often because one partner was manipulated or boxed in.

Alan Loy McGinnis

This greater love, this Jesus-love, honors the person it cherishes. It respects that person's right to live a separate—yet connected—life. It knows we have no control over a loved one's happiness. We cannot even interfere with a loved one's sacrifice as long as that is the loved one's desire. We must love standing by.

When we extend our limits through love, we do so by reaching out, so to speak, toward the beloved, whose growth we wish to nurture. For us to be able to do this, the beloved object must first become beloved to us; in other words, we must be attracted toward, invested in and committed to an object outside of ourselves, beyond the boundaries of self.

M. Scott Peck

Difficult? Indeed.

But rewarding. Not only to the beloved but to the one who loves. This Jesus-love frees us to go on loving, not only others, but ourselves. We have nothing to hide, and no regrets. We know we have honored what God created, instead of trying to tamper with it.

This greater love teaches us our place. We no longer try to play God. We know who we are: human beings, children of God, not fully formed yet, and there is only so much we can do. We love as much as we can, but no more. Then we let God love—through us.

The fully human person is in deep and meaningful contact with the world outside of him. . . . He suffers with the suffering, rejoices with the joyful. He is born again in every springtime, feels the impact of the great mysteries of life: birth, growth, love, suffering, death. His heart skips along with the "young lovers," and he knows something of the exhilaration that is in them. He also knows the ghetto's philosophy of despair, the loneliness of suffering without relief, and the bell never tolls without tolling in some strange way for him.

John Powell

The more we get what we now call "ourselves" out of the way and let Him take us over, the more truly ourselves we become. . . . It is no good trying to "be myself" without Him.

C. S. Lewis

It sees beyond its own need.

Jesus, near the end of His time on the cross, could look down upon His tormentors and ask God to forgive them. He could, in the midst of His own pain, answer the yearning in the heart of a thief on a cross beside Him:

And Jesus replied, "Today you will be with me in Paradise. This is a solemn promise."

(Luke 23:43, Living Bible)

...Jesus is the portrait of God. Here is the One who leaves the ninety-nine sheep safely in the fold and goes out after the one lost lamb—because He cares. By every word and deed, Jesus made it clear that His Father not only cares, but that no detail of any life is too insignificant for His loving providence.

Catherine Marshall

I know what it is to love with my entire being. I have been able to love without any thought for myself. But not at all times. I have also totally stopped loving because I had to look after my own needs. When I am hurt or troubled, I tend to turn away from those I want to love. I have wounds to nurse, problems to solve, and there doesn't seem to be any energy left over. I tell myself that the situation is only temporary, that when things are better I will get back to loving.

Enough of excuses!

We must learn to walk the Jericho Road—the road of service. On that road there lay a man who was wounded and needed help. Some came that way but passed by on the other side. One

36

man stopped and helped. Speaking of the one who helped,
Jesus said, "Go, and do thou likewise".

(Luke 10:30–37)

Some people walk the road of self-interest. They are opposed
to any sort of foreign aid, they refuse to give to the Community
Chest, the Red Cross and many other causes. They complain
about "too many collections." Such people have no sense of
obligation toward their fellow man. But Christ is not found on
that road. To walk with Him, we must remember His words: "I
am among you as he that serveth" (Luke 22:27). In order to walk
with Christ, one must surrender his selfishness.

Charles L. Allen

One day last summer I learned that a very dear man had died. Frank and
his wife Judy were married for more years than I had been alive, and they
were very close. Sensing Judy's despair at going on alone, I wanted to let
her know that I loved her, that I was there. I called her at home, and when
she answered her voice was strained. But the moment she recognized me,
she said, "I'm all right! I'm going to *be* all right, so don't worry about me.
But you—what about *you*? Are *you* all right?"

Frank had been like a father to me and I thought Judy was referring to my
own feeling of loss. I was so touched by her concern at such a time that I
thought I was going to cry. I didn't answer right away.

"Are you over the hurt?" Judy asked. That's when I realized that she was
talking about my grief over the death of a family member earlier that year.

"Yes, I am," I managed to say. "I've turned the corner."

"Tell me the truth now," Judy insisted. "I mean it—I want to know how
you are!"

Then the tears really came. There, in the midst of her own sorrow, Judy
was loving me—hard. I, who had called to comfort her, was being comforted
by someone who truly understood my need.

But what of Judy's need? How could she give to me without depriving
herself? Especially at such a time?

If thou art hungry, lacking heavenly food,
    Give hope and cheer.
If thou art sad and wouldst be comforted,
    Stay sorrow's tear.
Whatever be thy longing and thy need,
    That do thou give;
So shall thy soul be fed, and thou, indeed,
    Shall truly live.

Anonymous

Later, when the passing of time enabled us to talk about it, I told Judy how much her love had meant to me. "But how could you even *think* about me then?" I asked her.

"Think about you?" she said. "Oh, my dear child, that was when I really understood how you felt! And my heart just went out to you."

Those words describe so well the way Jesus loves. *His heart just goes out to us.* Not only when life is good or in the peaceful moments, but when He Himself is most in need.

Every man's need is your concern.

E. Stanley Jones

I do think that if people were to see, really *see* when they look, many things could happen. Very often we don't take notice of the people suffering near us. . . . And yet, consider the family I recently gave rice to after I heard they hadn't eaten for a long time. After I gave her the rice, the mother quietly divided the rice into two portions, and left the house. When she returned, I asked her where she had gone. "To my neighbor's," she answered, "with half the rice. Like me, they are also starving."

Mother Teresa of Calcutta

In terms of love, sometimes I have only half a bowl of rice to give to one who needs much more. Sometimes I am down to a few grains. And that is when I turn away, ashamed of my meager supply.

How blind I am to my own riches! I fail to see that out of my own need comes a powerful form of love which cries out to be given away: *I understand. I know how you feel. I am sharing this moment with you*. This is the way Jesus Christ is able to love us in His times of loss, as His own tears are shed, when He has been rejected, disappointed, deprived. This is the kind of love He gives us from the cross. And if you have ever experienced His understanding, felt His nearness, then you know how strengthening that love can be. It is all you need.

> I expect to pass this way but once; any good therefore that I can do, or any kindness that I can show to any fellow creature, let me do it now. Let me not defer or neglect it, for I shall not pass this way again.
>
> *Etienne De Grellet*

There will never be a time when you and I cannot love each other in this Jesus way. There will never be a moment when we cannot give to each other out of our own need.

> Grant that I may not so much seek to be consoled as to console; to be understood as to understand; to be loved as to love; for it is in giving that we receive, it is in pardoning that we are pardoned.
>
> *St. Francis of Assisi*

It appreciates the God within.

Question: Should we always put the needs of another ahead of our own?
Answer: Definitely not.

Imagine a grassy hill sloping gently away from the sea. It is late in the afternoon and you have been there for hours. But the time passed quickly. You had never heard anyone speak the way He did. You hung on His every word as He told you what it means to live as a Christian. Then He fed you, thousands of you, with a small portion of bread and fish that a boy carried in his basket—and you were filled. When He told you about God the Father, you knew somehow that everything He said was true.

But now He is tired. You can hear it in His voice. He stands and His friends press around Him almost as a shield. You don't want to let Him go. Suppose you never see Him again? What will you do without Him?

You must stop Him. Reach out to Him and clutch His robe if you can. Hold onto Him. Even if He can no longer speak, you must persuade Him to stay. His presence makes a difference in your life. Don't let Him go!

You can't believe it, but He brushes your hand away and His friends close Him off from you. They move toward the shore where their boat is pulled up on the wet sands. And before you know it, He is gone. You lose sight of Him as the boat moves off into the twilight.

Yes, Jesus could be abrupt. He was quite capable of saying "Leave Me alone." And He had His reasons.

He came to us for a purpose. He could—and would—spend Himself, but not on behalf of one person or one situation. He came to atone for us all; to meet and conquer death for us all. That was the God-created core of His life here among us, and He would not betray it. Not that He wasn't tempted —by the outstretched hand, by the empty bowl, by the mourning heart, the speechless lips and sightless eyes. "Lead us!" cried the multitudes lining His path wherever He went, and He must have wanted to deliver them from the Roman oppression. The temptation lay not only in the desperation of the people, but in the ease with which He could have delivered all of them. He was the Son of God! His power was unequaled.

And yet. . . .

There was within Him this core, this purpose for His life. And He would not compromise it—not for any other need on this earth.

> . . . I am in the Father and the Father is in me . . . I will ask the Father and he will give you another Comforter, and he will never leave you. He is the Holy Spirit, the Spirit who leads into

all truth. The world at large cannot receive him, . . . But you do, for he lives with you now and some day shall be in you. . . he will teach you much, as well as remind you of everything I myself have taught you. . . Take care to live in me, and let me live in you. . . . For apart from me you can't do a thing.

(John 14:11–15:5, Living Bible)

The Holy Spirit is the part of Christ that remains within us even when He must be elsewhere. If we love as He loves, then we too will leave a precious residue within our loved ones. Then, even when we cannot be in their presence, they will know we care.

But what a difference this Holy Spirit makes in the way we love. It means, first of all, that we must love the God within ourselves before we can love one another. We must build an intimate relationship with this inner Being. We must respect Him, learn from Him and let Him fill us with divine love. We must honor His needs as He seeks to shape us into a child of God who truly resembles its Father. And we must allow him to teach us how to recognize and love this same part of Christ within others.

Because of who you are and what you are, you can afford to believe in yourself and depend on yourself. You are easily upset when you lean on other people, but when you have learned to balance yourself on your own feet, you develop a stimulating independence. If God had wanted you to imitate someone else, He would not have made you in the first place. Never let yourself forget that you are a person God made and wanted at this time.

Charles L. Allen

You may be thinking that all of this talk about self-love involves a form of obnoxious behavior akin to egomania. Nothing could be further from the truth. Self-love has nothing to do with the sort of behavior characterized by telling everyone how wonderful you are. That's not self-love, but rather an attempt to win the attention and approval of others by chest-thumping behavior...It means the individual is evaluating himself on the basis of how others see him. Self-love means you love yourself; it doesn't demand the love of others. There is no need to convince others. An internal acceptance is sufficient. It has nothing to do with the viewpoints of others.

Wayne W. Dyer

This is a love to be spent lavishly, but never carelessly. Like Jesus, we must protect it from exhaustion. It is our steering mechanism to keep us on the course God intends for us, and so it must be valued most highly. It is our own personal source of Jesus-love which enables us to bring God's love into our world. No one, and no love on the face of this earth, must be allowed to direct it. Only God can. Surrender this love to anyone, or to anyone's needs, and we will lose it.

...I must try to be alone for part of each year, even a week or a few days; and for part of each day, even for an hour or a few minutes in order to keep my core, my center, my island-quality ....unless I keep the island-quality intact somewhere within me, I will have little to give my husband, my children, my friends or the world at large....woman must be still as the axis of a wheel in the midst of her activities; ...she must be the pioneer in achieving this stillness, not only for her own salvation, but for the salvation of family life, of society, perhaps even of our civilization.

Anne Morrow Lindbergh

Only recently did I learn how easily, and with the best of intentions, I could lose contact with my God-center. For several days I had been meeting one crisis after another in the lives of people close to me. One was in the hospital undergoing tests that might result in a grim diagnosis. Another, a teenager, was convinced that he had caused the separation of his parents, both of whom were my good friends. Another friend, a writer, was having trouble with a new assignment and kept asking me to read draft after draft the moment she pulled the pages out of her typewriter. I was also putting in long hours to make up for time I was losing away from my work. I was becoming irritable. I misunderstood what was said to me and detected criticism where none existed. I burst into tears for no apparent reason. The symptoms were obvious. I was running out of energy. *Don't worry*, I told myself, *soon you'll be able to rest*. It never occurred to me that I was also running out of love. I didn't know such a thing could happen.

Yes, it can. I found out when my friend stopped by one evening with one more draft of her article. I didn't even ask her into the house. "I'm tired," I said, standing in the doorway. "I can't talk now."

"Don't talk—just read," she said with the best of good humor.

Suddenly I felt very angry—at my friend, at her article, at her very presence in my life. I wanted to slam the door in her face. I was out of love. Or, rather, out of contact with my ability to love. My connection to the God within me was severed. It horrified me to be standing there with nothing to give to a person who meant so much to me.

I needed to spend a little time apart. That's all. I needed to get back in touch with Christ—because *I* needed to be loved by *Him*! Then I could pass it on.

But there was in my friend the residue of the love I had once been able to give to her, and she understood. I was too tired to explain, but she read the stress on my face and pressed my hand.

"Call me tomorrow," she said, "or whenever you're ready."

I don't ever want to come so close to running out of love again. I would rather take my cue from Jesus and let the God within me restore me with His love.

From Christ's behavior we learn three important things: (1) we can commit our resources to one another in spite of inconvenience and, at times, great cost; (2) we can commit ourselves in such a way to only a few people; and (3) we must also be committed to ourselves.

. . .The first few times my wife and children encountered me on my busyness, I had to admit that I was running too fast. That's when I had to make a clarification between my primary love for God and my devotion to the ministerial profession. The two were not the same. . . . If I really loved God, I would give my family what I should, and then I would give to my profession what I could. I find I have more to give to my profession when I enter it as a healthy, invigorated, and resourcing human being. However, when I get going so fast that I don't have time for my wife and children, I'm not nearly as effective as a pastor and consequently fail in my relationship with the congregation I serve.

Louis H. Evans, Jr.

Take my heart
and make it
Your dwelling place
so that everyone
I touch
will be touched also
by You!

Alice Joyce Davidson

It gives freely, joyfully, but will not be taken.

I know him well, the rich young ruler. I have approached Christ exactly as he did, many times. I have asked what I must do to be like Him and then decided that the sacrifice was too great. Or the price too high. Or the journey too hard and long for me to make on foot.

"Pity me," I would ask of Him. "I am not as strong as You are. Make an exception in my case."

He would have none of it. "You are as strong as you will allow Me to make you," He would tell me. And I would know, too, as He went on His way, that He loved me very much. I just did not love Him enough.

I also know the rich young ruler as a friend, because he has asked me often for my love. I have given it often, although he does not agree that this is so. He wants me to feel sorry for him—and I do. I pity him. I make allowances for him. That is not the same as loving him.

Friendship is a risk. There are usually no advance warnings about potential hazards. Sometimes I have no idea what's in the package but I reach out and take it anyhow, because God has created me for giving and receiving love. Any other way is far too lonely. But sometimes friendship's gift may contain perils, crises, transformations, complications I didn't count on in the beginning. What then?

I go right on loving and caring, but I learn that loving sometimes makes hard demands. Sometimes friendship withholds. Sometimes friendship must wound and wean for the health and wholeness of the other person—for the sake of balance.

Ruth Senter

Shy, indecisive, and struggling people may welcome or even invite us to provide for them. They may even say "I can't" when they really mean "I don't want to put out whatever is needed.". . .And we average persons are. . .very vulnerable, in fact, to such manipulation. It is more immediately gratifying to say, "Of course, I will do it for you," or to offer the advice, "What you really need to do is this. . . ." The right response in such cases usually provides much less immediate gratification. "Oh, come on, you can do it. . . .You have a good mind and you are capable of making decisions. What do you think you should do?". . .What people really need is belief in themselves, confidence in their own ability to take on the problems and opportunities of life.

John Powell

Jesus never denies anyone His love. But sometimes His love is rejected because it makes demands on the person who seeks it. Jesus asks quite simply that His love be put to good use. It is not a coin tossed into the cup of a roadside beggar. This greater love is meant to make up the difference between what we don't have and what we need to live abundantly. It is a tool thrust into our hands for the work we are to do in this world.

My teacher, Anne Mansfield Sullivan, had been with me nearly a month, and she had taught me the names of a number of objects. She put them into my hand, spelled their names on her fingers and helped me to form the letters; but I had not the faintest idea what I was doing. I do not know what I thought. I have only a tactual memory of my fingers going through those motions, and changing from one position to another. One day she handed me a cup and spelled the word. Then she poured some liquid into the cup and formed the letters w-a-t-e-r. She says I looked puzzled, and persisted in confusing the two words, spelling cup for water and water for cup. Finally I became angry because Miss Sullivan kept repeating the words over and over again. In despair she led me out to the ivy-covered pump house and made me hold the cup under the spout while she pumped. With her other hand she spelled w-a-t-e-r emphatically. I stood still, my whole body's attention fixed on the motions of her fingers as the cool stream flowed over my hand. All at once there was a strange stir within me—a misty consciousness, a sense of something remembered. It was as if I had come back to life after being dead. I understood that what my teacher was doing with her fingers meant the cold something that was rushing over my hand, and that it was possible for me to communicate with other people by these signs. It was a wonderful day never to be forgotten! . . . I think it was an experience somewhat in the nature of a revelation. . . . I wanted to learn the name of every object I touched, and before night I had mastered thirty words. . . . That first revelation was worth all those years I had spent in dark, soundless imprisonment. That word "water" dropped into my mind like the sun in a frozen winter world. Before that supreme event there was nothing in me except the instinct to eat and drink and sleep. My days were a blank without past, present, or future, without hope or anticipation, without interest or joy.

Helen Keller

Most human crises are events, and usually other events, rather than words, are needed to resolve them. Words may play a part, but by themselves they are insufficient.

Earl F. Palmer

I knew a teacher like Annie Sullivan. Her name was Hazel B. Evans, and when as a student you met her you had no idea what an effect she was going to have on your life. She was tall, slim, angular, quite proper looking no matter what she wore. Her eyeglasses had steel rims when everyone else had switched to plastic pastels. Her hair was always in place, more gray than brown. Her smile, while pleasant, was not going to light up your day.

But she was the hardest loving woman you were likely to meet. And there was nothing you could do about it because she was determined to love you into being your best self. Maybe *you* couldn't see that there was anything special inside you, but *she* certainly could.

Hazel B. Evans taught high school English and she ended up with a classroom full of incorrigibles from all the other teachers who washed their hands of them. She not only gave them a love for literature, but a love for life itself and all the wonderful things they could accomplish in it. A sullen, sarcastic boy from a troubled home went on to medical school. A pretty, giggly girl who had spent the previous summer in a home for unwed mothers decided to go on to graduation. And maybe college. Another girl, who had difficulty telling the truth, found a more constructive way to use her imagination through writing short stories—and sold one of them! A boy who stuttered got up enough courage to apply for a job writing sports news for the local newspaper—and got it. He also stopped stuttering.

Then Hazel B. Evans met her greatest challenge. He was a boy who couldn't read or write beyond the level of a second-grader. He had been promoted every year because his teachers felt sorry for him. He came from a family of high achievers, and his parents were ashamed of him. So there he was, a senior—and illiterate.

Hazel B. Evans flunked the boy, which meant he couldn't graduate. He could attend summer school and, if he passed the course, he would get his diploma. But he was old enough to drop out of school if that's what he wanted. And it seemed to everyone that it was. He was bitter. He was embarrassed because he couldn't graduate with his friends. He ranted. He raved. His parents complained to the school administrators. But Hazel B. Evans wouldn't give in. She was offered a compromise: give the boy a D-minus.

"He's better than that," she insisted. "He's got a brain in his head. Give him a chance to use it."

It was a standoff which only the boy could decide. And he surprised everyone. He went to summer school. He passed the course, but that wasn't all he did. He asked Hazel B. Evans to tutor him so that by the time he got his diploma he could read as well as if he had been a straight-A student—for real. On the day he was to receive his diploma in the principal's office, the boy asked Hazel B. Evans to accompany him. Her eyes got a little misty and she wiped her glasses carefully with a small linen handkerchief.

"That's very nice of you," she said. "But why me?"

"You cared," the boy said. "I could tell."

Caring is a very important part of love. It means that we don't just say we love someone and go on our way. We want that love to work in the loved one's life. We want it to become involved in the person's future. We want to be—responsible. The way He is.

It will not allow the beloved to manipulate the loving.

When I was twenty-five, I set out to find the father who had left my mother and me when I was two. He wasn't hard to locate because he wasn't trying to hide from me. He—and others in my family—thought it was best for him not to interfere in my life after such a long absence. My father was remarried and had other children. My participation in his life would have been, to say the least, confusing.

Nevertheless we had a deeply emotional reunion at the home of my father's sister, a warm and caring woman who had kept in touch with me all those years. I was struck by seeing a man I couldn't remember, yet one who looked so much like me. It was like finding a missing part of myself. There was something of that in his response as well. It would be good, we decided, for us to continue seeing each other now and then.

I never saw my father again. His new family objected to our having any relationship at all. It would be too painful to them, he explained to me by telephone. If he loved them, they told him, then he would agree not to see me again. And he loved them very much.

I understood how they felt. My reaction was the same. "If you love me, then you'll see me again," I insisted.

Poor man. I'll never forget the strained sound of his voice during our last conversation. Even the memory of it hurts. There must have been times when he resented all of us for asking him to prove what was quite clear—that he loved us. Why couldn't we just accept that—instead of trying to manipulate it?

Because that is the way we are.

And that is not the way Christ is.

Years ago Ralph Sockman wrote a fine book with the unforgettable title, *Love Is Something You Do*. In those few words he described the love we receive from God. There are no strings attached to it. We don't have to do anything, promise anything, be anything or perform in any way to be loved. We simply are. We can't even earn this magnificent devotion. It is ours, given to us without condition. Nor can we ever lose this love. We can flee from it, deny it, hide from it, and yet it remains. Wherever we are. It is with us, *within* us. We are loved. Like it or not.

We don't become holy by acquiring merit badges and Brownie points. It has nothing to do with virtue or job descriptions or morality. It is nothing we can *do*, in this do-it-yourself world. It is gift, sheer gift, waiting there to be recognized and received. We do not have to be qualified to be holy.

Madeleine L'Engle

In contrast, if we were to write a book about human love, we might have to call it, Love Is Something You *Use*—because that is what we try to do. We barter love to win approval, to get our own way, to improve our feelings about ourselves. Sad to say, we also use it to thwart God's will in the life of another.

We mean well. Love is important to us, so we try to hold onto it because we are afraid of losing it. Of course, the end result is that we often destroy love by abusing it.

When approval-seeking is a need, the possibilities for truth are all but wiped away. If you must be lauded and you send out those kinds of signals, then no one can deal with you straight. Nor can you state with confidence what it is that you think and feel at any present moment of your life. Your self is sacrificed to the opinions and predilections of others.

Wayne W. Dyer

One can embrace the object of one's love so strongly that one crushes him to death. Hate can kill, we all know. Policemen were invented to curb its murderous effects. But love also can kill, and there are no policemen who can deal with that.

Paul Tournier

This greater love is not a commodity. It is a miracle—it is God within us.

...For love comes from God and those who are loving and kind show that they are the children of God, and that they are getting to know him better....for God is love.

(I John 4:7–8, Living Bible)

For though we have never yet seen God, when we love each other God lives in us and his love within us grows ever stronger.

(verse 12)

The manner in which we love, then, identifies us. Do we belong to God? Or to someone—anyone—else? If we belong to God, this Jesus-love within us is at work in our lives. It is making us Christlike, teaching us how to think, feel, behave and do as He would do in our situations. And yet each of us remains an individual; each of us is shaped into a Christlike-you and a Christlike-me. There are no two of us alike, nor will we ever be copies of each other. No, if that were so, if we were to become identical models of Christ, then all we would have to do is follow a set of rules defining Christian behavior. God would be outside of us rather than within. But that is not the reason God created us. He wants each of us to be a separate image of His Son—because His Son lives for us all.

So that is the miracle of this greater love: it is God blending our separate selves into His own family by making us Christlike. If this love is allowed to work in our lives, then we, like members in a family, will keep our individual features and characteristics. But there will be no mistaking the basic family resemblance.

Jesus, aware of the divine nature of His love, would not allow anyone to use it for his or her own purposes. He would not allow anyone to attach conditions to His love, or to wrench it back and forth in a tug of war between persons trying to gain power over each other. Jesus was not deceived by "It's for your own good." He could be stern in his defense of loving.

My loving you can never be an abdication of my own self. I could possibly give my life for you out of love, but I could never deny my identity as a person. I will try to be what you need me to be, to do what you need done, to say whatever you need to hear. At the same time I am committed to an honest and open relationship. As a part of my gift of love, I will always offer my thoughts, preferences, and all my feelings, even when I think they may be unpleasant or even hurtful to your feelings.

John Powell

I think I am like Peter when it comes to loving. I always want those I love to be happy, to suffer none of life's heartaches. And I am convinced that I know what is best for them. Like Peter, I wouldn't want to hear Jesus telling me that He was going to die—and most cruelly. I would have looked for a way out. *Can't You hide, Lord, when they come to get You? Isn't there something else You can do to save us? Something that will let You remain here with us? I don't know what I'll do without You. If You love me—*

Dangerous words, those, even if they are not spoken aloud. I would have deserved the same rebuke Jesus gave Peter for trying to talk Him out of the cross:

Get thee behind me, Satan: for thou savourest not the things that be of God, but the things that be of men.

(Mark 8:33, KJV)

If we savor the love that is of God, then we do not have to demand: *If you love me, prove it!* But that is exactly what we are doing when we try to manipulate love. We don't need proof if we are truly loved. We know it. We feel it lifting us up, not putting us down. We gain strength from its support; we aren't weakened by its demands. It draws us closer to God and never comes between Him and us. And the minute we hear words such as "If you love me, then—" we had better beware. Because, whether the rest of the plea is uttered or silent, its meaning is clear: *If you love me, then you will put me ahead of God in your life.*

Lastly, I cannot ever let you use or manipulate me. We must love persons and use things. I am a person, not a thing. To let you use me would be no act of love, either for you or for myself. Please understand that I will never set myself up as your judge. I cannot now nor will I ever be able to read your intentions. I can know your intentions only by asking you. But I will never allow your temper tantrums or your tears to compromise my com-

52

munication. If I feel suspicious of you, I will confront you with my feelings. If I feel hurt by something you have said or done, I will say "Ouch!" When you affirm or console or congratulate me, I will forever be visibly grateful to you.

John Powell

If I could, I'd write for you a rainbow
And splash it with all the colors of God
And hang it in the window of your being
So that each new God's morning
Your eyes would open first to Hope and Promise.
If I could, I'd wipe away your tears
And hold you close forever in shalom.
But God never promised
I could write a rainbow,
Never promised I could suffer for you,
Only promised I could love you.
That I do.

Ann Weems

There is another, more subtle way we sometimes try to barter love. We offer something priceless in exchange for it: *I will do whatever you ask—if you will love me.*

Sound familiar? It should, because each of us, at certain moments, yields to this impulse. We want to belong, to be included, acknowledged, which is the same as saying we want to be loved. And so we become, or offer to become, what we believe others want us to be in order to be granted their love. We choose our friends, our neighborhoods, our schools; we dress, spend our money, even speak, in particular ways; we cut corners, break laws, forsake the truth and overlook corruption—because "everyone is doing it," and we want to belong to "everyone." We want "everyone" to love us. Young people call it peer pressure.

When we offer to perform in exchange for love, we are as manipulative as the person who demands, "If you love me, prove it." We simply speak in a softer voice. But we are attempting the same kind of barter: *I will put you ahead of God in my life, if you will love me.*

Jesus often found Himself in situations that tempted Him to offer such an exchange. He was a Man of taste and was comfortable among cultivated persons. He could dine with the best of them and never use the wrong fork. Yet He could bless the unmannerly interruption of a prostitute who seized the right to worship Him as the Son of God. He was criticized; love and approval were withdrawn. Who knows if He was ever invited back to that house again. But—who cares!

He also was a Man of vigor and earthy strength. His disciples were rough-cut men used to struggling with the forces of nature, and He could show them new, more effective ways to cast their nets and maneuver through the storms. Yet, in the darkness of an orchard on the night before He was to die, He could admit His need of their company in His loneliness. No matter that they didn't understand and promptly fell asleep—He asked them. He exposed His fears and was vulnerable to this band of devoted but uncomprehending tough guys.

Jesus never tried to be anything that He was not. He didn't have to. He knew He was loved—and by whom. Never did He allow anyone but God to direct His love. And neither must we.

This greater love within us is our inheritance from God. It is meant to be given, freely, but never exchanged.

When it comes to forming a truly intimate relationship, I have one role model: Jesus Christ. He accepts me—unconditionally—and in spite of my fears of rejection. He makes no effort to control me or our relationship; we are bound by mutual love and regard. It's going to take me some time to follow his example, but I can't think of anything better to do with my life. I trust him, even with my fears and apprehensions. I know now that he will never let me go. At times I offend him and he reacts in righteous anger. He confronts the wrong I have done, yet he never stops loving me. At those times when I make him proud by accepting his will over my own, he commends me—but he makes it very clear that my obedience isn't the reason why he loves. So it does me no good to argue that I am too dumb to be loved; nor can I claim that any kind of achievement has earned me his love. He simply does love. And that is the way I want to relate.

James S. Evans

It relates honestly.

I am not perfect. Neither are you. Can we possibly love one another? Indeed, if—

we admit that we have our faults,

we love what is truly lovable in each other,

we deal directly with what is not.

I can't love all of you. Not if I am honest with myself. I will not like everything you are, in every situation. Neither can you love all of me because there are bound to be facets of me that you can't accept. If we try to love everything about each other, allowing no exemptions, we will be doing love a disservice. Love must be totally honest or it will end.

I used to think that a Christian had to love everything about a person. So I tried. I tried to love the negatives as well as the positives in everyone I knew. I thought that if I could only understand why some persons did things that were hard to take, I could love their faults, too. Sometimes understanding worked. But sometimes it made matters worse because I didn't like what I understood about the person. And there were times when I couldn't understand at all.

Why, for instance, did a friend who was always there in my worst of times, become distant and uncaring in my better times? Why did another friend *always* ask me for advice—and then *always* turn around and do something else? Why did a friend who gave me much good advice resent it when I disagreed with him?—once! Why did a friend lie? Why did a friend who seemed so trustworthy let me down? Why does a friend, who is so fond of me, say such terrible things about everyone else? And will she say them about me, too? Why, when I want to achieve something, does a certain friend tell me all the things that could—and, in her opinion, *will*—go wrong?

I blamed myself when I wasn't able to love a friend's faults. I thought I wasn't enough of a Christian. Then I had a talk with a woman who was, to me, very much a Christian.

"What do you do," I asked her, "when you can't love everything about a friend?"

She smiled rather wistfully and said, "You love what you can—just the way Jesus does." When she saw the look on my face, she laughed. "There's probably a lot about you and me that Jesus doesn't like. But He doesn't cancel us out."

Of course, she was right. Imperfections do not have to end a friendship. But—what does love do about them?

For one thing, love doesn't complain. Love doesn't grit its teeth, force itself to smile at the beloved—and then go telling someone else what is wrong with the beloved. That isn't honest. Nor is it love.

When love finds something in the beloved that it simply can't live with, it confronts the problem openly. It is like Jesus, asleep in a boat that put out onto calm waters, suddenly awakened by the frightened cries of His companions. The water has become rough and strong winds are hurling waves against the boat, shoving it to one side and another, threatening to capsize it. The men are afraid. They cower and tremble, whimpering to each other. Yet they are the men Christ has chosen to learn from Him and then to carry on His work through the world. Without them, His sacrifice will stop at the cross.

If I had been in His place, I would have been thoroughly disillusioned. I would have tried to get the boat to a safe shore and then left the others. Oh, there is much I would have told people about the friends who let me down, about the cowards who spoke so bravely. I would have complained loudly. For I *have* been in His place. But I have not been *like* Him.

Jesus knew, when He chose His disciples, that they were not perfect. Perhaps He knew from the beginning just what their faults were, but more likely they became apparent to Him as He lived among them. The important thing is that He did not cancel them out as His friends when they disappointed Him. He loved them for their strengths, and there were many; and He confronted their weaknesses without apology.

Another of his disciples said, "Sir, when my father is dead, then I will follow you."

But Jesus told him, "Follow me *now*! Let those who are spiritually dead care for their own dead."

Then he got into a boat and started across the lake with his disciples. Suddenly a terrible storm came up, with waves higher than the boat. But Jesus was asleep.

The disciples went to him and wakened him, shouting, "Lord save us! We're sinking!"

But Jesus answered, "O you men of little faith! Why are you so frightened?" Then he stood up and rebuked the wind and waves, and the storm subsided and all was calm.

(Matthew 8:21–26, Living Bible)

All was calm. And so it is when we stop trying to force ourselves to love what is not lovable in each other.

Some people speak up and let difficult people know exactly how they feel. They fight back. Because "fight" has hostile overtones, perhaps it is not the best word to use here. "Assertiveness" might better describe what is meant. In any case, fight is the opposite of flight. Instead of holding back and keeping silent in the presence of a difficult person, we speak up and let him or her know exactly where we stand.

. . . Being assertive does not mean pouring boiling-hot water on a difficult person—even though we are steaming. When done properly, it becomes top-level communication. Whether it should take place face-to-face at a public meeting or in private conversation depends upon the circumstances.

Andrew Costello

I am certain I am like those who were in the boat with Christ. I assume, as they did, that being in His presence means guaranteed serenity. I don't think the disciples were unconcerned about the stresses of life; they had *been*

57

there. They had eked out a living under the shadow of a tyrant. They were survivors: adaptable, resourceful, toughminded—hopeful even before they had a reason to hope. They were responsible. Answerable to authority. Nose to nose with life and death. But—here was this wonderful Person of promise in their midst and they assumed that all would be well. They—and I am one of them—rejoiced in their lives.

The trouble is, they didn't really understand what goodness and mercy are—and neither did I.

> . . . Discipleship means sometimes it's going to rain in my face.
> *Ann Weems*

I remember the shock I experienced when I discovered that Christians do not always get along with each other. I had thrown myself into church work and was serving on committee after committee. I wanted "to get things done" and had little or no patience with those who dragged their feet. And feet were dragged. Also, some good people had little patience with my impatience. At times we came close to exchanging angry words, but we always stopped short of confrontation. It seemed, somehow, unchristian to shout at each other. So we swallowed our displeasure and were meticulously polite with each other. Consequently nothing got done. Until one night, at a meeting of the official board, a man I had always considered the epitome of diplomacy and tact suddenly threw his scratch pad across the table and stood up, glaring at the rest of us.

"Jesus wouldn't have put up with this!" he said. "And neither should we!"

Two things happened in quick succession:

We all gasped.

Then—we all realized that he was right.

Jesus would have been angry—and He would have brought His anger out in the open where the rest of us could deal with it.

Now—does this kind of behavior seem unchristian? It did to me, at first. Then I went back to my Bible and began reading it as if it had just been written—that day, that moment, in this life of mine. Because one of the miracles about the Bible is its timelessness. It was valid then—and it is now. It also offers to each of us a personal message for each day of our lives.

For instance, John tells us that "Christ became a human being and lived here on earth among us. . . .We have all benefited from the rich blessings he brought to us." (John 1:14, 16, Living Bible)

I don't know where I ever got the idea that Jesus Christ was a misty creature whose transparent feet never touched the earth. Yet I did think of Him in that way. Perhaps it is because I am convinced He is the Son of God, and I am in awe of His divinity. Nevertheless I tend to overlook His humanity, and in doing so I deprive myself of a blessing.

Jesus is God speaking to the man in the street. He is God meeting me in my environment, a human environment. . .He met life as a man. He called on no power for his own moral battle that is not at your disposal and mine. He did perform miracles, but only for others and in answer to human need. He performed no miracles for himself. His character was an achievement. Everything he laid before men in the words spoken on the Mount had gone through his own soul. They were livable, for he was living them.

E. Stanley Jones

Jesus is like you. He is like me. He is like every other human being you or I have ever known. He is all of us and He is each of us. He lives this life each of us is living. And He enriches it with His presence.

So if Jesus had attended our board meeting—and I believe He did—He might have found it not unlike some of the gatherings He attended in the synagogue. We were trying to be "nice" instead of being human. We still try. We think Christians ought to be soft-spoken, all of one opinion, happy and problem-free.

Well, we are not. Nor was He.

Back to the board meeting. . . .After the outburst of one board member the rest of us earnestly tried to deal with our differences. We were clumsy. We were still trying to be "nice." We thought we could disagree without hurting anyone. While such a thing may be possible, it certainly wasn't for us that night. We ended up tongue-tied and went home because it was getting late.

What we didn't realize—and what I began to learn from reading the Gospels—is that we can't simply decide to behave in a certain way and then do it. Something is missing.

Could it be goodness and mercy? I wondered. I knew it was time for me to come to terms with these words.

When I think of goodness, I think of Christ. He was and is perfection. He is everything a Christian wants to become—and I use the word *become* deliberately. We are not perfect, we all know that. We may never be perfect, although we hope that isn't so. But we are striving to be perfect. As Keith Miller says, we are *becomers*. We are constantly in the process of becoming more like Christ, and this is one of the reasons why life is so precious. It gives us the opportunity to be remolded in His image. So "if at first we don't succeed," we keep on becoming. And that, to me, is goodness in a person.

Mercy? Again I think of Christ and especially during the years He spent in this world. Here was Perfection meeting less than perfection everywhere He turned. Yet He was able to love us, flawed though we are. He could see beneath the marred surfaces to the goodness that was *becoming* within us. And that special insight to me, is mercy.

So it was no wonder that none of us at our board meeting was able to reveal our true feelings without inflicting wounds. We, each in our own way, may have been striving for goodness, but we had no Christlike love for that which was flawed—including ourselves. In fact, we were as hard on ourselves as we were on each other—because we did not offer mercy to our own imperfections. We shouted them down, hid them under politeness, and growled fiercely at anything or anyone who threatened to expose them.

Who—me? Angry? How dare you! I don't even want to discuss it, thank you.

We weren't able to say to ourselves: "So, you're upset? Well, basically you're a nice person, and being upset doesn't change that. Besides, maybe you have a reason to be angry. Why don't we talk about it?"

Being unable to offer mercy to ourselves, we were therefore unable to give it to others. Result: division. No love. Nothing. All we could see in each other was a different point of view—the marred surface.

Then our feisty member called us together at his home one evening. At first it seemed like a pleasantly sociable event until he singled me out, looked me right in my eyes and asked, "Do you love Jesus?"

"Of course I do!" I blurted out, feeling somewhat offended at being picked on.

"Then love the Christ you see in me, and tell me why you disagree with me!" he said. "And when you do, I'm going to love the Christ I see in you."

There they were, goodness and mercy. And they made all the difference. I could debate the man's ideas without attacking the man. So could the others, because he went on to confront each one of us in the same manner. By the end of the evening we had compromised on our differences and I think we all felt we had some valuable new programs under way. But more than that, we shared a kinship with each other that we had never experienced before.

We were in touch with the Christ in each of us.

> The healthy relationship stays healthy not only because you let your negative feelings out when they occur. It is also healthy because you let your beloved do the same. Your friends are fortunate if they do not always have to be good company with you, if they can be crotchety and cranky when they need to be, knowing that you wil not reject them for it.
>
> *Alan Loy McGinnis*

This greater love is not blind. It does not ask us to love what is not lovable in each other. Nor does it ask us to make excuses for what is inexcusable. But it does urge us to let each other know—directly—when something is unacceptable. This is not criticism; this is love. This is not saying, "I don't love you anymore because of what you have done." Or, "I won't love you unless you change." This is saying, "I love you, but I can't love what you are doing."

Dishonesty always has a way of coming back to haunt and trouble us. Even if I should have to tell you that I do not admire or love you emotionally, it would be much better than trying to deceive you and having to pay the ultimate price of all such deception, your greater hurt and mine. And you will have to tell me things, at times, that will be difficult for you to share. But really you have no choice, and, if I want your friendship, I must be ready to accept you as you are. If either of us comes to the relationship without this determination of mutual honesty and openness, there can be no friendship, no growth; rather there can be only a subject-object kind of thing that is typified by adolescent bickering, pouting, jealousy, anger and accusations.

John Powell

A few years ago a friend of mine, whose name is Rebecca, was involved in a complicated legal matter and asked her brother, Vaughan, an attorney, to advise her. The two of them were very close and could talk for hours on end, but that was quite different from discussing a lawsuit.

Right from the beginning Rebecca noticed that Vaughan was uncomfortable during their conversations. He frowned often and kept getting up from his desk to pace the room. It wasn't like him at all. Finally one day he exploded in anger. "Rebecca," he said, clenching his teeth, "you keep interrupting me when I'm trying to explain a point of law! I can't stand that! As a lawyer I'm trained to say what I have to say—and then let the other person speak."

Rebecca says she wasn't hurt, but she was embarrassed. She didn't realize she was interrupting her brother so often. She thought she was just asking some questions as they came into her head, which she always did when they talked.

"I'm sorry, Vaughan," she said. "I'll try to keep still."

She did try. Very hard. And mostly she succeeded. But there were times when she needed to ask a question in order to understand what Vaughan was explaining. And it seemed he never *would* stop talking. The questions began piling up in Rebecca's mind, and so did her resentment.

She raised her hand—"like a kid in school," she told me, laughing. Vaughan stopped in midsentence, scowling.

"Vaughan, I can't stand it when you don't give me a *chance* to speak," Rebecca said. "Now I'll try not to interrupt if you'll try not to talk for so long without stopping. Do you think that will work?"

It did. Very well. "I think each of us became better listeners by speaking up," Rebecca said. They also became better friends.

It will not always be so. Honesty in love does not assure honesty in return.

Now Jesus was in great anguish of spirit and exclaimed, "Yes, it is true—one of you will betray me." The disciples looked at each other, wondering whom he could mean . . .

So I turned and asked him, "Lord, who is it?"

He told me, "It is the one I honor by giving the bread dipped in the sauce."

And when he had dipped it, he gave it to Judas, son of Simon Iscariot.

As soon as Judas had eaten it, Satan entered into him. Then Jesus told him, "Hurry—do it now."

None of the others at the table knew what Jesus meant. Some thought that since Judas was their treasurer, Jesus was telling him to go and pay for the food or to give some money to the poor. Judas left at once, going out into the night.

(John 13:21–30, Living Bible)

We may, like Jesus, love a Judas Iscariot who cannot meet our level gaze, who shrinks from our honest refusal to accept what is unlovable, and who will not settle for being loved for the Christ that is in him.

What then? Can we love such a person?

It does not ask for more than the beloved can give.

When I was a child, and even beyond that, certain special days aroused a great deal of anxiety in me. Valentine's Day was crucial; after that came my birthday. On those days one received greeting cards—or one didn't. Yes, we sent cards to commemorate other special days—Christmas, the New Year, Easter, Mother's Day, Father's Day, and a sprinkling of others in between. *But*—on Valentine's Day and on your birthday you find out how much you are loved by those you love. Or, you *think* you do—because you gauge your lovableness by the volume of mail you get. A lot of cards means you are getting a lot of love back in return for all you have been giving. A few cards—or worse, none—mean you haven't been giving much love and therefore don't deserve much in return; *or* you aren't getting anything in return for all the love you have been pouring out. And that hurts.

> We are all clutching at something or some collection of things that give meaning and substance to our lives. But sooner or later our grip on those things tends to weaken. Or the things themselves disintegrate. The root cannot bear so much weight for so long a time. We ask too much of both the root and our hands.
>
> *Earl F. Palmer*

It does hurt when we aren't loved as much as we love. According to the words of a song that was popular years ago, the most important thing in life is to love and be loved in return. I think most of us subscribe to that theory. I think most of us love in that manner: expecting our love to generate love in others, which will then be given back to us. *If you don't love me as much as I love you, that's the end of it!* And if that were the way Jesus loved, then the New Testament would be one long record of rejection—of us by Him.

He was not, and is not, loved in return—at least not nearly as much as He loves. He does not ask for more than we can give, and He is well aware of our limitations. This Jesus-love asks only to love—and, yes, it does ask.

Imagine that! God asking us if we want His love! Not asking us if we want Him to love us—He does, has, always will, and that is His own decision. We can't change it, or cancel it out. *He loves us*. But He does not impose His love upon us. He asks us if we want to receive it, if we want to be in a loving relationship with Him. He holds out His hand to us, but it is our decision whether or not to clasp it in ours. This is very different from the way we love each other, and it will take time to learn from Him.

He could love a Judas Iscariot even though He knew of the man's deceit. He could confront His betrayer and then share His bread with him, all the time asking nothing in return. Christ's love was not dependent upon the love He got in return—and ours *must* not be. Nor did His love always generate love in the beloved; on the contrary, it could arouse hatred, fear, contempt. It could, and did, lead Him to the cross. And even from the cross He could go on loving us.

Sometimes we too are going to love more than we are loved. Sometimes the only thing we will get out of loving is the loving itself—and that is not a small matter.

> I have told you all my feelings; I love you with all my heart. Any coldness still between us is not because of any lack of love on my part, but because your love is too small and does not reach out to me and draw me in.
>
> *(II Corinthians 6:11–12, Living Bible)*

We have become deeply concerned these days with the ways we express love to each other. We want to know—through touch, specific words, attention, gestures and deeds—exactly how much we are loved and by whom. When we love someone we want that person to acknowledge receipt of it, with appreciation—or else give it back if it doesn't happen to be the correct size and color. This is all very good for those who can express love. But not everyone can.

Some of us find it difficult to draw near in love. We are like Martha busying herself with all kinds of things in the kitchen, while Christ sits in the adjoining room with people pressing close around Him. Nevertheless we Marthas love Him, in our own way. And while He may be disappointed because we are not within reach, He loves us, too.

Some of us are like Peter, boisterous in our expressions of love, exaggerators who cannot possibly live up to all the love we promise to bestow. But we love Him, too, and He knows it.

There are some Nicodemuses among us, as well—we who are too reserved to love Him openly. We come to Him in private, after hours. We discuss love, we analyze it in quiet conversations. Yet He understands. He accepts whatever we can give.

This, then, is how we must learn to love each other: expecting nothing in return, and being overjoyed with whatever is offered. It is the loving that counts—because when we truly, and freely, love one another, then God is living through us. He is anointing the world with His love—through us. And this is return beyond measure.

> ...Let us practice loving each other, for love comes from God and those who are loving and kind show that they are the children of God, and that they are getting to know him better....for God is love....For though we have never yet seen God, when we love each other God lives in us and his love within us grows even stronger....anyone who lives in love is living with God and God is living in him. And as we live with Christ, our love grows more perfect and complete....
>
> *(I John 4:7–8, 12, 16–17, Living Bible)*

Remember, this is not love in the ordinary sense. It is not touching, speaking, being physically close or sharing another's life, although any of those things may be present. But they are not essential to this love, and they may very well be absent. Even the beloved may be absent, because this greater love does not require the beloved's presence.

> You love him even though you have never seen him; though not seeing him, you trust him; and even now you are happy with the inexpressible joy that comes from heaven itself.
>
> *(I Peter 1:8, Living Bible)*

What is required, and what distinguishes this Jesus-love, is a *regard* for the beloved. A caring about what happens to the beloved. A sense for what the beloved is thinking and feeling. An acknowledgment of the beloved's identity—an appreciation of what the beloved is, but also a tender compassion for what the beloved is not, and may never be.

It took me many years and many agonized gropings to learn that I could love a person who did not—and does not—love me back. The person is a close family member, a woman I have known since childhood, and I am not the only one she has tried to love and couldn't. Her problem is that she herself grew up in an unloving environment and she wants so much to *be* loved that she cannot give love. She also doesn't recognize love when it enters her life and usually finds a reason to turn away from it.

So—how was I to love this woman? And why did I even want to try?

Because she was family, and I thought there was something wrong with me if I couldn't love a close relative. And also because she was truly a likable person underneath all that bristly exterior.

Unfortunately, the more I tried to love her, the harder she pushed me away. The rejection hurt, but I kept trying because I blamed myself for the failure. *Failure*! Yes, that's the way I thought of our relationship. It had failed—because I loved her and she didn't love me back. I was, of course, thinking of love in human terms. As far as I knew, love had to be reciprocal or it wasn't love.

Like most other people, I have experienced a few other failures in loving, but this one troubled me the most. It haunted me. It even angered me and in my mind I kept asking questions: Why won't you love me? *Why!* Is there something wrong with *me*? Is there something wrong with the way I love? Can I love *anybody*? *Ever*?

You can see where I was headed: toward a very poor self-image. All because I wasn't getting loved back. My identity was at stake: *If you don't love me, then I must not be worth anything*.

Not so. I realize that now.

I know—now—that I am worth a great deal. For one thing, I was created, and that means something. I am a part of God's miraculous gift of life. I am touched by His will for me to exist, to be a person. I am, *therefore*, an inheritor of His love. I am one of those Christ saved from death. There is an immortality in me, and I finally understand what that means. It means that Someone most precious, Someone far better than I am, walked where I am walking now, experienced my own loneliness, my own need for love, and understood. That most precious Someone reunited me with my true family in a bond that will never be broken. I am a child of God, and I am loved beyond all reason. But that is an outright gift. It was bought with intense suffering and sacrifice, none of it mine. I don't possess such love. I can only receive it—and pass it on.

This gift is mine to give to others—and this is why I can now love without being loved in return. I am absolutely filled. My cup overflows with more love than I ever imagined was possible. And so, of course, I must give it away! This is its essence. Like the wheat-white sourdough base that my great grandmother kept in a snug corner of her painted cupboard, it has to be used, given to neighbors and friends, taken from constantly, or it will become stale, lifeless.

There are moments in our lives so lovely, they transcend earth, and anticipate heaven for us. This foretaste of eternity has made clear to me the perpetual and all-embracing service that friendship should ever be.

Helen Keller

...You are in my heart forever and I live and die with you. I have the highest confidence in you, and my pride in you is great.

(II Corinthians 7:3–4, Living Bible)

I wish I could spend time with my troubled relative. I wish she and I could talk often and easily instead of struggling through our occasional awkward conversations. I wish we could hug each other. In short, I wish she could love me back. But she can't and I am finally able to accept that inability. Yet I do love her. I don't force myself on her, but I keep in touch. She knows that if ever she needs me, I am there. I pray for her and about her. I am conscious of love going out from me to her; I need nothing in return. We don't have to see each other; *regard* keeps her close to me.

God doesn't pursue us or force His love on us, either. He allows us to limit the relationship with Him, and I am sure we often grieve Him by the distance we keep. Yet He is there, and if one day we should decide to close the gap between us, we will find that it doesn't even exist. That is the way love really is.

> Do all the good you can, by all the means you can, in all the ways you can, in all the places you can, to all the people you can, as long as ever you can.
>
> *John Wesley*

It will lay down its life for the beloved.

Do I have to?

Can't I love someone without giving up my life for that person?

Of course. We do it all the time.

We all can remember a time, perhaps more than one, when we were so much in love that we would have died—*gladly!*—just to make that person happy. But we really didn't mean it.

I can also remember visiting a hospital for wounded veterans some years after World War II was over. When I left, I was stunned from the horror of seeing so many ruined, forgotten human beings. I felt so guilty about being physically whole that, for a moment, I wished I could die to make even one man well. But I didn't really mean that, either, and the wish didn't last long. It came from outrage, not from love.

A few years ago, when my mother had to undergo the amputation of her leg, both my stepfather and I wanted to take her place, even to die for her, if that would have helped her. We both meant it because we loved her that much. But our dying wouldn't have helped her, or cured her disease, and we knew it.

None of these experiences was a deliberate consent to give up one's own life so that another might live. They were not acts of Jesus-love. But Jesus did more than lay down His life for us. His death accomplished something worthwhile, and that is the meaning of sacrifice: "For ye are bought with a price" (I Corinthians 6:20, KJV). Through His own suffering love, He did for us what we could not do for ourselves: He delivered us from evil and brought us back to God—forever. Death itself was ended in His dying, and a new life, life without death, began. Out of this ending came a beginning: that is sacrifice. It is not throwing away one's life—for life is precious—but using it for all it is worth. And the purpose had better be a good one.

What was needed was the ultimate Word. Then the Great Simplification took place. The Word became flesh.
E. Stanley Jones

I am a more sensitive person, a more effective pastor, a more sympathetic counselor because of Aaron's life and death than I would ever have been without it. And I would give up all of those gains in a second if I could have my son back. If I could choose, I would forego all the spiritual growth and depth which has come my way because of our experience, and be what I was fifteen years ago, an average rabbi, an indifferent counselor, helping some people and unable to help others, and the father of a bright, happy boy. But I cannot choose.
Harold S. Kushner

The letter lay, fragile and stained, on top of the pile. It was hard going through my mother's things. Missing her was still so new. I looked at the date. It had been written by a friend to my mother in 1939, shortly after my father died.

"Dear One," it began, "it hurts so terribly, doesn't it? Accept the pain if you can. Say, 'Yes, because I loved and now lost, I must cry for a while. I must hold this ache of loneliness within myself and say, this is the price I pay for having loved. I will accept this price and pay it in gratitude for the love I was blessed to know, for I would not have wanted to be without that love. I will pay this price, God, and I thank You for the wonderful years we shared.'

"I think He must have cried on the day that His Son hung dead on the cross, don't you think so? Don't you think that because He, too, is familiar with tears, dear friend, He is especially close to you right now?

"I weep with you, and my love surrounds you. Please write and let me know your plans, and if there is anything at all I can do to help."

I folded the letter and slipped it back in the envelope, grateful for this healing message from the past.

"Thank you for the wonderful years, Mom," I whispered. "Of all the women in the world, I'm so lucky *you* were the one God gave me. Yes, it was worth the price."

Doris Haase

A friend of mine, a woman in her forties, recently allowed surgeons to remove one of her kidneys and implant it into her sister, who would have died without it. My friend might have died during the operation, and she will have to live more carefully now. But her sister has a chance to survive. That is Jesus-love.

Larry, a tall, spindly seventeen-year-old who lives around the block from me, is hardly the hero type. He's a quiet, deep-thinking boy, and it takes a long time to get to know him well and find out how much people mean to him. He was coming home on his bike one day and saw his little brother dashing out into the street after a ball and into the path of a car. Larry didn't have much time to decide what he wanted to do. He only had time to love. Pedaling furiously, he rammed his bike into the side of the car and the driver stopped. Larry had a broken leg, and he'll always walk with a limp, but it could have been worse. His brother was safe. The sacrifice was worth something.

This past winter, on an icy road along a river, a car with a young couple in it skidded off the road and crashed through the guard rail into the water. The car sank out of sight as traffic stopped and people rushed to the river bank. One man kicked off his boots and jumped in. He came up briefly and then dove down out of sight. Everyone said he would never come up again. The cold and the current would finish him, they said.

But he did come up. Twice. He saved both passengers of the car. That night, when he was interviewed on the six o'clock news, he was asked the inevitable question: "What went through your mind as you dove in?"

"I knew God would have done the same for me," the man answered.

"Have you ever done anything like that before?" the interviewer asked, not comprehending the answer.

"No. I guess I never had the opportunity before." Jesus-love can be quite matter-of-fact.

Suffering is part of the portion of living and in order to walk with Christ, we must not only bear the sorrow, we must so use our sorrow as to make it a blessing.

A young mother saw her little daughter suffer a severe fall and die a few days later. The mother's world went to pieces. She secluded herself in anguish and despair. Then one day the voice of God seemed to say to her, "Have you ever thought of the many girls who have no mother and need one? Why don't you use your love for them?" Her name was Josephine Webb, and she rendered magnificent service from then on. She learned to walk the road of suffering with Christ.

Charles L. Allen

These are heroic examples, and I am not heroic by nature. I live quietly, simply. Does that mean I will not be called upon to lay down my life? Will I be spared this most difficult act of love?

Oh, no. For if we choose to love as Jesus loved, then we will be called upon to suffer. And suffering will come to us in the quiet corner of a sunny room as surely as it will on a cross in a place of public execution.

A single parent, a father with a severely retarded son, brings the boy home every weekend and holiday. It isn't easy. The boy keeps repeating the same few sentences over and over, and he requires a lot of care. Friends say the boy would be better off if he remained in his special school all the time, but the father disagrees.

"It's a fine school," the father says, "but it's an institution just the same. Maybe my son isn't capable of realizing it when he's home with me, but I can't help hoping it makes some kind of difference in his life. If bringing him home lets him know he's loved, then it's worth doing."

A nurse took a leave of absence to look after her mother-in-law, who is terminally ill. The two of them never got along and they still don't. "I don't mind," the nurse says. "I want her to be with her family as long as she can. It makes me feel good. And I want my husband to have this time with her."

Is a life of love, which involves a permanent and unconditional commitment to the happiness of another, really the way to personal satisfaction and human fulfillment?

John Powell

The comfort is not a sickly sentimental thing—it is not the wiping of tearful eyes, but the re-enforcing of the heart... Senseless suffering is not comforting—it is dulling, disintegrating. This, then, must be a suffering of a particular quality—a gladly chosen pain. This brings comfort. There is nothing so absolutely blessed as to be able to suffer well.

E. Stanley Jones

...We know that we belong to the Lord. Our allegiance is given; it is committed; we cannot turn back. That is not to say that we may not slip, that we may not transgress, that we may not weaken. But in Surrender, something fundamental happens. After that, nothing is ever the same.

Emilie Griffin

Don't confuse this kind of love with martyrdom. Laying down one's life is not always an act of love. It may, in fact, be an act of hate. Or protest. Or, worst of all, spite. It may be done out of desperation—quickly, impassioned, with nothing gained. Martyrdom ends where it begins: with the death itself.

Similarly, if your husband or wife died, you may hang on to one of your sons or daughters to the point that his or her marriage is dominated by the incessant demands you make for time and attention. You *control* this son or daughter by means of your grief. Thus your grief ceases to be a suffering from which to recover; it becomes a tool with which to stay in the center of a son's or daughter's (usually a daughter's) attention. Your grief becomes a test of affection. That is, if this child loves you, he or she will respond to your every twinge of unhappiness. Without intending to do so, you have actually become a cruel taskmaster. Have done with such a way of life.

Wayne E. Oates

Or think of Peter, drawing his sword and swinging it clumsily as soldiers came to arrest Jesus in the orchard. Peter was not a swordsman and he missed his mark. He cut off a man's ear. But he was ready to swing again and surely he would have been cut down by the other soldiers if Christ had not intervened. *No*, Christ told him, *don't lay down your life. Not now. It won't accomplish anything.* At that moment, Peter displayed courage, no doubt about it. But he was not attempting to lay down his life out of love.

That would come later, long after Peter was brought face to face with his own weakness, long after his Master demonstrated what suffering love could do. It was only when Peter took up Christ's command to bring His message of love to all the world, knowing very well that he too would suffer death for it, that Peter began to lay down his life for a friend. He did it not out of rage or passion, but deliberately, knowing what he was sacrificing and accepting the loss with grace. He went beyond human love—into the divine.

I cannot consciously "sacrifice" for you even if I love you. If I love you, what I might do for you will flow from my heart because you are *in* my heart. I do not believe Jesus hung on his cross thinking: "Now, I'm sacrificing for them." He hung there pouring out his blood for us because we were *in his heart*. This does not mean he did not suffer. His agony drove far beyond anything we could comprehend. Not only did his body experience the torture of the most brutal kind of physical death, he did battle with all the selfishness and sin all men had ever committed or would ever commit. We cannot understand this. It is vanity to try. But this combined, two-pronged agony of body and spirit did not make him feel righteous. He *was* all righteousness. In the midst of his suffering, Jesus felt *natural*, because, to God, it is natural to love. The death of Christ did not change the heart of the Father toward us. The death and suffering of Christ revealed what the Father's heart had been like all along.

Eugenia Price

Suffering is not *putting up with*. It is *trying to make a difference in*. It is doing what someone cannot do for himself and offering up what is most precious to ourselves. And there are no guarantees of success. This kind of love takes a terrible risk when it stakes its very life on the possibility that the beloved will gain from its sacrifice. Christ is still waiting to find out what each of us is going to do with this life He bought for us.

Do we have to love this way? No one says we must. The choice is ours.

Now those that "mourn" are comforted. The strange thing happens that those who deliberately take on themselves trouble and pain in behalf of others find happiness—they are comforted. The most absolutely happy people of the world are those who choose to care till it hurts. The most miserable people of the world are those who center upon themselves and deliberately shun the cares of others in the interest of their own happiness. It eludes them. They save their lives and they lose them.

E. Stanley Jones

Truly I have looked into the very heart of darkness, and refused to yield to its paralyzing influence, but in spirit I am one of those who walk the morning. What if all dark, discouraging moods of the human mind come across my way as thick as the dry leaves of autumn? Other feet have traveled that road before me, and I know the desert leads to God as surely as the green refreshing fields and fruitful orchards.

Helen Keller

And what do we get out of it? Nothing—at least, not by human standards. We will not be thanked. Our sacrifice may not be commemorated or even recalled by those for whom it was offered. But that is what it means to be a disciple. It is the experience of giving ourselves so completely to God that He can use us to make a difference in His world. It is feeling Jesus Christ breathing through us.

4

THE MYSTERY
OF THE OPENING DOORS

God opens many doors to us—and sometimes I wish He wouldn't. I find it difficult trying to decide which one He wants me to enter.

I also wish God would open some doors that insist on remaining closed in spite of all my attempts to push them open. I like to think I have a right to go where I choose.

Such is the dilemma of a disciple. What does God want for us? And why don't we always want the same things?

When a door doesn't open

"I refuse to believe that God wants me to go through the rest of my life as a blind woman!" Ginny said, her mouth tightening in a hard line. She was twenty-three, pretty, and very much alone in the world. Now a door had closed in her face, the door of sight. She had been examined by specialists, all of whom agreed she would be totally blind in another year. They didn't know why. And there was no cure.

"What will I do?" Ginny said. "I've already had to give up my job. What kind of work can a blind person do? How will I live? How can I earn some money?"

They were enormous questions and they would have to be considered one at a time. Blind men and women *do* earn a living. Financial aid *is* available

77

to them for emergencies and special education. But Ginny would have none of that kind of talk.

She knew better. She would pray. She would take God at His word and *insist* on His help. She would knock at that closed door until it opened and she could see again.

She prayed. She went to more doctors. She ate foods and took vitamins said to improve vision—which might have worked if Ginny had any vision left. But she didn't. In less than a year she was totally blind. I lost touch with her when she moved out of her apartment and left no forwarding address. It was as if she had been swallowed up by her own darkness.

Then I saw her again a few years later. She came toward me, walking along a busy city street filled with shoppers and office workers on their lunch hour. I stopped, amazed. She was more beautiful than ever and she walked with her head held high and there was a smile on her face. Alongside her, fitted with a special harness, was a large dog, a guide dog, maneuvering her briskly along the crowded sidewalk.

She stopped when I called her name and we threw our arms around each other. We had to talk hurriedly because Ginny was on her way to class. She was teaching Braille to adults who had recently lost their sight.

"I was depressed for a long time," she told me. "That's why I moved away. I tried to move away from God, too, because I was mad at Him. Then I realized that He didn't do this to me. He was hurting just as much as I was because I couldn't see. So I asked Him if there was something else I could do besides see. That's when I began to accept the fact that I was blind. I learned how to walk with a cane, and then I decided a guide dog could help me move around even more. When I tackled Braille, though, I ran into a problem. It's awfully hard to learn. So the harder I tried, the more I wanted to teach other people how to read with their fingers. That's what I'm doing now—and I have to run or I'll be late for class!"

A door had closed. And another had opened.

> The great temptation of life is to follow our own desires, to make our own plans, to be guided by our own wills—and to hope God is willing.

But suppose God is not willing? Then we have only one of two choices: to renounce God's will and follow our own, or to renounce our own will and follow God's. And most of the time we must make that choice without fully knowing what God's will is. That requires more faith than some people have. It requires more courage than some people have. It never is an easy decision to make. Jesus' struggle was so great that sweat like great drops of blood began to pour from His face to the ground.

Charles L. Allen

. . .One does not have to understand to be obedient. Instead of understanding—that intellectual understanding which we are so fond of—there is a feeling of rightness, of knowing, knowing things which are . . . .then we can have the courage to go wherever we are asked to go, even if we fear that the road may take us through danger and pain.

Madeleine L'Engle

When a closed door opens

Ginny wasn't wrong to fight for her sight when she learned she was losing it. Sometimes we have to be like Jacob and wrestle with God. It strengthens our faith: "I will not let thee go, except thou bless me" (Genesis 32:26, KJV). Or we must dare to speak with the honesty of the father who brought his son to Christ for healing. The boy had been unable to hear and speak since childhood and, obviously, specialists had been consulted. As a last resort, perhaps, the father had brought his son to Christ's disciples—and they couldn't heal him. Now he knocked again at a closed door. "Oh, have mercy on us and do something if you can," he said to Jesus (Mark 9:22, Living Bible).

Not a great statement of faith, was it? But very much like our prayers of desperation. Full of *maybe's* and *if's* and *I'll try anything, Lord!*

"*If* I can?" Jesus asked. "*Anything* is possible if you have faith" (v. 23). And we can imagine God saying that to us more often than we care to admit. Doubt has a way of perforating our faith.

And then the distraught father uttered what many of us may feel but hesitate to say, especially to our Lord: "I *do* have faith; oh, help me to have *more*!" (v. 24).

Did you think a Christian has no doubts? Did you suppose a Christian never trembles as he sets out upon an unknown path in faith? Did you think a Christian never wondered whether God was near? Whether God heard him? Had compassion for him? Judged him not?

Oh, my dear fellow Christians, you are a miraculous mixture of faith and doubt—because you are of this world and also of God. It cannot be otherwise; you are made from His breath and the dust of the earth, and God acknowledges this conglomeration. Now it is time for you to do the same.

That is why some doors open and some doors close. That is why some—maddeningly—almost close and keep opening again. There is in your life a constant struggle between your will and the will of God. And He will not overrule you. He endowed you with the freedom to choose, and if He is to have you, He will only have you by your own free choice.

So knock at a closed door. Pound on it until your fists are swollen and bloody. Don't be polite. God does not stand on ceremony. Raise your voice. Cry out until you are speechless and your throat aches. And then, only then, turn away and seek a door that *will* open to your knocking. There always is one.

Conscious of the greatness of God—beyond the measure of our minds—and of the power of sin which dulls our perception, the true believer seeks his road step by step, combining faith with the most realistic self-criticism. He is always on the lookout for some sign sent from God to confirm his faith, or else to correct some error in it.

Jesus himself spent years at the workbench before assuming his mission. He himself told of his inner struggles in the desert and in Gethsemane. He went every morning to seek God's commands in prayer.

Paul Tournier

But—which door?

There have been times in my life when I have pleaded with God to close a door in my face. Not just one door, but all of them, except the one He wants me to enter. Life would be so much easier that way. Then I would know, for sure, that I was not only seeking but finding God's will.

But no, the doors keep opening, more of them all the time, and just when I think one may be closing—it opens again, perhaps not by much, but enough for me to stick my foot in. Sometimes I try to go through half a dozen doors at one time, ending up exhausted, confused, angry at God for putting so many possibilities before me. I *know* He knows what is best for me. I *know* He knows how I can make the best use of the abilities He gave to me. Why doesn't He tell me?

Actually He does. But in His own way.

After I was married for several years it became obvious, to me at least, that I wasn't able to have a child. My husband and I had prayed for a family. We consulted several doctors and none of them could pinpoint the problem, much less solve it. To me, that was a door closing. In a sense, it was a relief, because the years of frustration had worn me down.

Until then I had never taken a career seriously. I had worked in publishing and developed a few editorial skills. I had tried to write, but not seriously; it required a dedication I wanted to give to other areas of my life. I was planning to be a busy mother and I didn't want to get sidetracked.

Well, it didn't appear that I was going to be a mother, so I decided to make myself useful in other ways. I *thought* I was bringing God into my decision. I prayed often, asking Him to lead me wherever He wanted me to go.

And then I got a wonderful idea!

A seven-year-old boy who lived in our neighborhood used to come and play with my dog after school—and he was breaking my heart. He couldn't read or write. He tried so hard, and his parents did everything they could to help him, but he couldn't make head or tail out of the simplest word. Put a picture in front of him and he understood its meaning immediately. He could put his disassembled Christmas toys together by following the diagrams. He could think, all right. And because he was intelligent and sensitive, he was aware that there was something different about him. Something wrong. Something that made him withdraw into himself more every day until finally my dog was the only creature who could communicate with him emotionally.

Today, of course, we would know what to do for such a boy. But in those days the term "learning disability" wasn't even used. Children were said to be "slow" readers. Some were diagnosed as retarded when they weren't. In other words, they were problems, and no one knew what to do about them.

Because of my interest in my young neighbor, I looked into the problem. I heard about a new field of education, remedial reading, which, it was hoped, might help slow readers. Only a few universities offered such training, and only on the graduate level. That's when I got my wonderful idea. I would go back to school and take my Master's degree in remedial reading. I would work with children like the boy who was breaking my heart.

I was elated! I was absolutely convinced that God was opening a door to me, and I rushed to get to the other side.

Application forms! I hate them! Yet I filled them out carefully and compiled all the other records universities require. I needed one more personal reference and I decided to ask the editor of a publishing house where I worked on a part-time basis. That's when another door opened.

The editor, an exceptionally talented woman, was leaving, she told me. She had accepted a job in another part of the country. Did I really want to go back to school? she asked.

Not really. But I had to if I wanted to teach remedial reading.

Was that really what I wanted to do?

Why? I asked.

Well, she wanted to recommend me to replace her.

I was flabbergasted! Of course, I wanted the job. I loved publishing. I loved being an editor. I wanted to learn everything I could about it. I never dreamed I would have the opportunity so soon.

Two weeks later I was agonizing over a decision that had to be made. I had been accepted by the graduate school I wanted to attend, and I was offered a job as an editor. On the one side was a special little boy who was losing his grip on reality. It was too late to help him, but there would be others. On the other side was a yearning to help communicate thoughts and ideas. If God didn't want me to teach children to read, why didn't the university turn me down? If I was selfish to want a job as an editor, why did the publisher keep making it so appealing? Please, God, close a door in my face!

He didn't—because He wants us to make up our own minds. He sees more clearly than we ever will, He has His preferences about what we shall do with our lives, but He will not bend us to His will. He would not do that to His only begotten Son. He wants us to be His by choice. Even the wrong choice.

Whatever my decision might have been, I know now that God would have done all He could to help me carry it out. If I made a mistake, He would help me to learn something valuable from it. If I fell on my face, He would help me to my feet to start over. He would—and will—keep opening doors. We are the ones who must close some of them.

I closed the door to a Master's degree and a career as a teacher of slow readers. I might have been a good teacher. I don't know. But I do know that I have not regretted my decision to go into the publishing world. There was a talent for writing that needed to be developed and I was given the opportunity to do it. Along the way I have been given many other opportunities for talents I most certainly do not have, and I found that out quickly. I failed at many endeavors. Occasionally I went through the same open door so many times that I began to doubt my reasoning powers. But eventually I got the message and closed the door myself.

I used to think a disciple was a person who knew where he or she was going. Not so. A disciple is a person like you or me, wanting to follow Christ, wanting to serve God in this world, but not knowing how. A disciple is someone who gets very confused by all these opening doors and all these choices in life. He does not want to make the wrong decision. He does not want to play games with life. He wants it to mean something. But—and here is the difference—he trusts *God* to give his life meaning. He dares to walk through the open doors because he trusts God to help him find his way back if he makes a mistake.

I believe in God, the Almighty Ruler of nations, our great and good and merciful Maker, our Father in heaven, who notes the fall of a sparrow and numbers the hairs on our heads. I recognize the sublime truth announced in the Holy Scriptures and proved by all history that those nations are blessed whose God is the Lord. I believe that the will of God prevails. Without him, all human reliance is vain. With that assistance I cannot fail. I have a solemn vow registered in heaven to finish the work I am in, in full view of my responsibility to my God, with malice toward none; with charity for all; with firmness in the right, as God gives me to see the right.

Abraham Lincoln

Before I can listen to God in prayer, I must fumble through the prayers of words, of willful demands, the prayers of childish "Gimmes," of "Help me's," of "I want. . . ." Until I tell God what I want, I have no way of knowing whether or not I truly want it. Unless I ask God for something, I do not know whether or not it is something for which I ought to ask, and I cannot add, "But if this is not your will for me, then your will is what I want, not mine." The prayers of words cannot be eliminated. And I must pray them daily, whether I feel like praying or not. Otherwise, when God has something to say to me, I will not know how to listen. Until I have worked through self, I will not be enabled to get out of the way.

Madeleine L'Engle

You and I might have been one of those along a Galilean shore some centuries ago when a Man with a compelling personality offered us the most outrageous challenge: "Follow Me." Where? How? For what?

Do you think we would have asked? Do you think we would have demanded credentials? I doubt it.

PART II

MEETING LIFE'S DEMANDS

1

IT'S OKAY TO BE HUMAN

Are you uncomfortable with the word *disciple*? Do you feel as if you're wearing someone else's clothes—a hero's or a heroine's, perhaps?—and they're too big for you? Are you self-conscious about all your faults and shortcomings? Are you trying to make yourself over? Into what?

In my early days as a Christian I was painstakingly critical of myself. I wanted to look like a Christian, speak like one, and certainly to behave like one. As I looked around me for some examples to follow, I found a lot of other people doing the same thing: looking at each other and criticizing what they saw. Trying to fit the image of a disciple can take up a great deal of time and energy.

My emotions caused me the most concern. They seemed too earthbound for a disciple. I thought a Christian shouldn't be too much of anything— happy, sad, excited, anxious, worried, angry or content. After all, *disciple* comes from *disciplined*, doesn't it? Which means we ought to keep a tight rein on all our human tendencies. Doesn't it?

I couldn't have been more wrong. I was following the lead of Christians who were as lost as I was. Then I met a remarkable, outrageously human and most genuine disciple. Her name was Helen Steiner Rice.

She certainly didn't fit my image of a disciple. She was a tiny, vibrant woman given to quirky gestures and far-ranging moods. Her bright red hair was piled high up on her head in an elaborate arrangement of curls, and on top of that she almost always wore a hat. Not an ordinary hat, mind you, but a maze of tulle and lace, feathers and flowers.

"My hats are my trademark," she used to say matter-of-factly when she caught you staring. Not that she needed a trademark; her poetry was read and loved by people all over the world. But that wasn't what Helen meant by a trademark. Her hats made her easy to spot when she walked into a department store in Cincinnati, where she lived for many years, and she got the attention of a salesclerk right away. Helen didn't like to wait. Not for anything.

She didn't like some other things, either: rudeness, broken promises, thoughtlessness, lies, putting on airs, greed, laziness, carelessness, to name a few. And when she didn't like something, she let you know it. Her eyes flashed not only an extraordinary intelligence, but downright anger, utter disappointment, impatience, disapproval, and you'd-better-stop-what-you're-doing-right-now!

She was known for some eccentricities in her lifestyle: For riding the company bus to work every day when she could have afforded a taxi and gone in later. "I like to ride with the people I work with," was her reason for getting up at the crack of dawn to catch the bus. For tearing apart an editor's arrangement of her poems for a book, *every time*—and for putting them back together in a better way, *every time*. "Well, I know more about these things than you do," she used to say. And she was right. For telling her boss at the company where she worked that she didn't want the raise he planned to give her. "I've had plenty of raises," she remarked when someone asked her if she realized what she was doing. "When I need more money, I'll ask for it." She lived well. Comfortably. She was a consummate business person and had fought hard to get where she was. But enough was enough. And, as she said, when she wanted more money, she made no bones about it. She knew what she was worth.

Helen had a temper, and people who had been in its path steered clear of it. If you called her up and she was in a bad mood, she'd tell you she didn't want to talk and she'd hang up. But when she wanted to talk, it was a gift. You learned something that stayed with you.

I'll never forget the time I quit my job when I thought I was denied a promotion because I was a woman. That was in the days when people were only beginning to use such words as "women's liberation" and "equality under the law," and I was very touchy about any evidence of sexual bias. Helen happened to call me on the day I resigned, and immediately she sensed something was wrong with my life. For the first time in our long friendship, she was quiet. She let me do the talking. When I finished, she said, "I'm going to send you something. Read it."

I expected a letter. Instead I received a photocopy of a newspaper clipping that went back to a time before I was born. In a two-column article, featuring a photograph of a young, lovely, Helen-eyed woman, was a description of a lecture she gave to a group of businessmen. In no uncertain terms, she told them that if they were as smart as they thought they were, they would soon realize that they were missing out on a wealth of talent by denying women the same opportunities they gave to men in the business world. And the audience loved her!

So did I. Who else but Helen Steiner Rice could have pointed out so clearly, yet so efficiently, that the problems I was encountering had been around for a long time? Who else could have convinced me that, although I shouldn't give up, I really could be a little more patient? This from an impatient woman—but, as I said, she was a genuine disciple, and she gave to me out of an awareness of her own need.

Helen taught me many other things, but the most valuable lesson I learned from her is that a disciple is a human being. In fact, that's what a disciple is all about: a person looking to Christ as his or her example. That's the way Helen lived, and, believe me, she wasn't heroic. She was fully mortal, emotions and all. She just kept trying to improve the way she lived her faith. She was thoroughly at ease talking to God and she always asked Him what He thought she ought to do. Sometimes she found His instructions very hard, but she did her best to follow them. Not that she felt righteous. Oh, no. She was disarmingly aware of her mistakes, of her quick rebukes and her impatience, and even when her reactions seemed justified, she sought God's forgiveness. She was thoroughly persuaded that God loved her enough to put up with her quirks. She not only knew what unconditional love really meant; she dared to count on it. And that's the way *she* loved. She could bite your head off and then bind the wound.

No one could ever ask Helen to write a poem—because as far as she was concerned it was God who gave her the talent, and she never wrote a word until He was comfortable with the verses forming in her head. If God didn't like the way the poem was taking shape, then it wasn't written. Only when God was ready did the words come together. Beautifully. Sometimes Helen wrote several poems one after another. Sometimes she didn't write at all. It depended on when God was ready. That was one area of her life where Helen could be patient.

In the last Christmas card she sent she said good-by to her friends in the world. She knew she was going to die.

I've written many Christmas messages for friends throughout my life. But none has ever meant as much as the one I send this year, for there are no words to tell you what knowing you has meant.

With happy memories, I've shared my love with all of you, and I've written many Christmas verses in my "eighty years." And it was always a great joy to remember you and tell you how much your friendship meant to me.

As I look forward to "WIDER FIELDS OF USEFULNESS," I can only repeat what I've said for all these years . . .

"YOU HAVE ALWAYS BEEN A PART OF MY LIFE! AND NO WORDS I WRITE CAN TELL YOU HOW MUCH MY ENTIRE LIFE HAS BEEN A PART OF ALL OF YOU!

"I LOOK FORWARD TO MEETING YOU ALL IN GOD'S TOMORROW. MAY GOD REUNITE US IN HIS HEAVENLY HOME WHERE LIFE IS FOREVER AND OUR FRIENDSHIP BECOMES PART OF GOD'S KINGDOM!"

Helen Steiner Rice
Christmas, 1980

A few months later, when she was very ill, I thought it might cheer her up to get her mind on her work. "Are you going to write a poem soon?" I asked her.

"No," she said, her voice weary, "I asked God if He wanted me to write some more verses, and He said no, it was time for me to rest." And that's what she did, a week later.

Helen taught me what a disciple is. Not a perfect human being, not a hero or a heroine, but an ordinary person who is coping with life—not according to the world's rules, but in the manner of Jesus Christ. A disciple doesn't always succeed—but, even in the failing, something is gained. A part of God's Kingdom is brought into the world. And that's what we are here to accomplish.

2

HOW CHRISTIANS COPE

When I gave my life to Christ, I thought He was going to change it. He didn't. He changed *me*. And *that* made a difference in my life.

Is it better? Yes. But not easier.

Am I happy? Infinitely. But happiness is not what I once thought it would be.

How is my life different? It isn't mine; it's His, and it took some time for me to understand what that means. I had to learn that only by giving myself could I receive Jesus Christ.

And my faith? What happened to it? I'm living it. With Christ's help. With His love. With His presence. And with His assurance that whatever I can't do, He can.

I am not perfect. I continue to make mistakes and He continues to forgive me. Sometimes, when I find it difficult to walk with Him, I go my own way. I always come back and He always welcomes me.

Every now and then I succeed in giving Him so much of my obedience that I feel His thoughts in my own mind. I see with His eyes. His strength enables me to do what I never believed was possible. For some brief moments I have been able to love as He loves. It has been the greatest blessing I have ever known.

Meeting life as a Christian does not mean we will avoid problems. We will know ups and downs, we will confront hard decisions and unexpected changes. We are not immune from stress and the ravages of anxiety. New experiences will come our way and we will not always know what to do about them. We will hold joy close to us and hope it will last forever; we will weep when it does not. We will share our lives with many, and when some bonds are broken we will know pain that does not end. We are so very human.

But we are more than that. Coping with the complexities of life is only the beginning of our story, and we will go on from there. Because for the Christians there is a beyond. It's the discipleship that grows out of the coping, it's the giving of ourselves to others, that brings us closer to God. That is our goal.

And there are steps along the way to that goal. They will take us through challenges that demand more courage, insight, understanding, love and suffering that we have. That is how we will discover the incredible power God is waiting to give us.

FINDING THE KINGDOM WITHIN:
Ministering to Your Inner Needs

God is here within us and He gives us
strength to endure life's pressures....

WHEN YOU'RE LONELY

"I watch, and am as a sparrow alone upon the house top."

(Psalm 102:7, KJV)

There it is again, the feeling that no one cares, that no one even knows
you exist. Where you are has nothing to do with it. You may be in a room
filled with people or you may be eating dinner by yourself. You feel cut off.
Disconnected. You're lonely.

> You—sitting in the pew next to me—
> I'm lonely.
> You'd be surprised at that, wouldn't you?
> How could I be lonely with all the family and friends
>   I have?
> I'm not lonesome, I'm lonely!
> I'm lonely deep down where it hurts.
> I want to reach out to somebody and say:
> This is me. This is really me.
> But everybody passes quickly.
> They're all so busy....
>
> *Ann Weems*

Loneliness hurts. It makes us feel we don't matter, and that makes us angry. We want to matter. We want to share our lives with those we love and cherish. We want them to share themselves with us. But something gets in the way.

Before we can enter into a close relationship with another person. . .we have to acknowledge the fact that we can't make it in this world on our own. For most of us, this is very difficult to do because in our society we are taught to be, or to appear, self-sufficient. We're not supposed to share our problems or admit that we've been hurt because strong people aren't supposed to have any problems. The corollary is that if we do expose a need or a wound, we are weak.

. . .If there were any person of whom we might say, "He didn't need anybody," it would have been Jesus Christ. Yet in several instances he admitted his need so that his disciples could give help to him. And toward the end of his life, when he was wrestling with the knowledge of his impending death, he said to three of his disciples, "Come pray with me because my heart is heavy." He needed their presence, and even though they disappointed him and fell asleep, the point is that he asked them. . . .

It is the weak who say, "I don't need you." They are simply trying to appear strong when actually they are not.

Louis H. Evans, Jr.

As Christians we can taste some of God's infinite understanding; but we must learn to talk to one another, to tell who we are, and why we are the way we are, and who we hope to become. Tolerance grows in our Body because we have had honest glimpses of those inner men. Sensitized through the work of the Holy Spirit, we become able to breathe deep draughts of compassion. Our hearts become opened to Him, and opened to one another, and His love is able to flow through us to our brothers.

. . .Loneliness is a human condition. Each of us has to learn how to be a friend and how to make and keep friends.

Karen Burton Mains

Sometimes we let our fears or our self-inflicted judgments of inferiority shield us from taking the risks and facing the challenges of a full life. We substitute "I can't" for "I won't even try."

John Powell

Loneliness is the child in us, afraid of the darkness of an uncertain world. It is the infant crying out for the parent, longing for the comfort of strong arms around its vulnerable body.

Don't be ashamed of this child in you. It is a wonderful part of yourself. It connects you to God. It brought Jesus to His knees in Gethsemane when He suddenly felt alone among His closest friends. And the child in Him cried out to His Father in Heaven and received the protection of a Parent's presence.

When the child in you cries out, bring it to your Father. Then, when you understand you are truly loved, that you really matter, you will be able to speak to another of your need. And if that other cannot hear you, you will go on to yet another, because you are no longer afraid of being turned away. You know you are lovable.

The Lord is my friend and my companion.
How can I ever be lonely so long as he is with me?
He walks along a country road with me and opens my senses to loveliness never noticed before. The glitter of gravel beneath my feet, a tangle of sun-sweet grasses, a dust-colored toad—all are remarkable and fresh.
He accompanies me along the busy streets. . . .The crowds don't overwhelm me. I can look into their passing faces and briefly, joyously know them—for the Lord is within them too.
I can go to a party where all are strangers, yet I am happy and at ease, for my Lord is also there.
I can come home to an empty place, a silent place, yet the Lord enters the room with me and fills it.
I will not hide within the Lord, for I am in the world and of it and his warm living people are dear.

Yet other friends, other companions, he will send me in abundance so long as I keep him near.

And whenever others fail me or my spirit needs escape I can turn to the Lord and be at peace.

Marjorie Holmes

Learn to fill your days up, one day at a time. Don't try to fill the void all at once. Find your loneliest day; fill it half up with fun and friends. Then, concentrate on one other day. Once you have done this with several days in your week, you'll find that the quality of your life has improved, and much of your depression will have turned to joy and much of your anxiety—your cover-up for loneliness—will have gone.

Toby Rice Drews

You know, also, that you have something to give as well as something to ask. When someone else is lonely, you will recognize it. You will understand why that person cannot reach out to you. And you will do the reaching. Your inner child and the other person's child, by clasping hands, will end the loneliness.

There is ample reason for man to blame his inability to love on factors apart from himself. . . . It's easier and safer for him to sit alone, even if he feels a natural urge to relate to others, than run the risk of being shunned. He elects to remain silent, alone and lonely and states as his basic defense, "What if I approach him and he turns away?" He seldom asks, "What if I extend my hand to another and he reciprocates with, 'Yes, please join me.'"

I recall an evening. . . . I saw a gentleman at a nearby table, sitting alone. . . ."Why don't we ask him to join us? He seems so alone," I said. "I know what it means to be alone in a room full of people."

"Leave him be," was the consensus of the others. "Perhaps he wants to be alone."

"That's fine, but if I ask him, he'll have a choice."

I approached the gentleman and questioned whether he would like to join us or if he would prefer being alone. His eyes lit up with surprise. He accepted happily.

Leo Buscaglia

Don't turn away from any man saying that you have nothing to give or lend—you have. If you are Christ's you have something to contribute to that man's need.

E. Stanley Jones

Prayer for the Reader

Sometimes I can be standing next to a friend, Father, and feel a great distance between us...sometimes I want to cry out, but have no voice. Only You perceive my uncertain presence. Only You hear the words I cannot bring to my lips. You see me watching You from the roadside, and You reach through the throng to take my hand and bring me close to You. You let me walk with You part of the way, until my step is strong—and then You send me along another road looking for others who have lost their place in the crowd.

WHEN NO ONE UNDERSTANDS

"I will give them hearts that respond to me."

(Jeremiah 24:7, Living Bible)

Tell me what you feel—that's what everyone says. So you tell them. At least, you try. You reach deep down inside yourself to find the words that fit what is going on in your life.

And what happens?

"Don't worry, you'll get over it."

"I know, I know. I went through the same thing, only worse. I'll tell you what I did. . . ."

"What you need is to get your mind on something else."

In other words, *Don't tell me about your problems—I have enough of my own.*

We have a pain—maybe a small one, maybe it's pretty big—and we want to ease it by telling someone about it. Maybe if we can hold it at arm's length and get some perspective on it, we'll begin to figure out what we can do about it so it won't hurt so much. The people we know keep coming up to us, putting a hand on our shoulder or grasping our hand in theirs and saying, "Hi, how ya doing?" But it really isn't a question, and they really don't want to know the answer. "Hey, you look great!" they tell us without actually looking and go on their way without seeing the pain that throbs just below the surface of our faint, wan smile.

. . .When we wave a flag of trouble and our loved ones go past without stopping, it makes us angry—and rightly so. We feel rejected, disappointed, unimportant, and it doesn't take many of those experiences in life to make us decide, "If that's the way they feel about me, I'll take care of it myself!" And so we withdraw.

. . .When someone puts up a distress signal, that doesn't mean we have to step in and solve his or her problem. All we have to do is be aware that the problem exists and listen for the sound of pain. "Wait, what was that you said? How do you feel about that?" can do a lot to help another person get his problem out in the open. Then *he* can do something about it.

Louis H. Evans, Jr.

No, we can't always put ourselves into words. Sometimes there *aren't* any words to describe us. So we can't make ourselves understandable, can't explain what is going on inside us. The most frustrating part of wanting to be understood is that it is up to someone else to do the understanding. Even in those rare times when we can describe ourselves to another, that person then has to be able—and willing—to feel what we are feeling. Because understanding is sharing. It is Jesus listening to the courteous, almost formal pleas of a Roman centurion who asked Him to restore a dying daughter to health—and hearing, underneath the mannerly words, the fear and desperation of a loving father. It is knowing what cannot be put into words.

He knows we have groceries to buy, rent or payments to make on our houses, clothes that are necessary, expenses for the children in school, bills of every sort to meet. Not only that, He knows we have desires and wants beyond our bare necessities. We are not wild beasts. We want some of the pleasant things of life.

Charles L. Allen

God *does* understand. Because He is one of us. He doesn't expect us to be noble—only human. That's the way He made us.

When we seek understanding, we aren't looking for answers. We don't want to be told we are right or wrong to feel as we do. All we want is to know that someone else has felt the same way. We don't want solutions to a problem, we may already have them. We don't want to be told that what we feel isn't really important; to us, it is. We certainly don't want to be told that we shouldn't feel the way we do.

Job needed sympathy more than he needed advice, even good and correct advice. . . He needed friends who would permit him to be angry, to cry and to scream, much more than he needed friends who would urge him to be an example of patience and piety to others. He needed people to say, "Yes, what happened to you is terrible and makes no sense," not people who would say, "Cheer up, Job, it's not all that bad."

Harold S. Kushner

We want to know that we are not alone. That someone else has been where we are now.

We need to feel more to understand others.
We need to love more to be loved back.
We need to cry more to cleanse ourselves.
We need to laugh more to enjoy ourselves.
We need to see more other than our own little fantasies.
We need to hear more and listen to the needs of others.
We need to give more and take less.
We need to share more and own less.
We need to look more and realize that we are not so different
    from one another.
We need to create a world where all can peacefully live the life
    they choose.

Susan Polis Schutz

Perhaps we are weary from trying to explain ourselves. Perhaps we shrink from the prospect of one more preoccupied gaze, one more slight shrug of the shoulders, one more too-discreet glance at a clock.

Perhaps we must seek not so much to be understood, as to understand. Because in sharing another's feelings, we too are *being* shared. In understanding, we too are *being* understood. We are intruding ourselves into a situation another person is experiencing, which takes some courage because our presence may not be welcome. But if we remain quiet, if we don't insist on finding a way out, if all we offer is the beating of our human heart and the steady warmth of our loving presence, we may actually be accomplishing that rarest of achievements: understanding. We may also be making it possible for someone else to understand us.

Jesus was no stoic. His heart was moved to pity by the ragged mob that came to hear him (Mark 6:34); his heart was ripped in hurt at the death of his friend (John 11:33); his heart lurched with affection toward the young man who walked away from him (Mark 10:31). Jesus shows us a God who takes risks with his heart and invites us to do likewise.

The quality of God's mercy is the point of the parable of the prodigal son (Luke 15:11–32). The hero of the story as we know, is not the son but the father. Jesus tells this story to teach us about the possibility of repentance, yes, but even more, to tell us that we can always repent, for there is always a merciful father. The father of the prodigal son is God our Father. And like that anxious, doting father who ran out every day expecting his son's return is our Father in Heaven, who runs before us with mercy every day. He is no scorekeeper; he is in the game and risks his love with us constantly.

We have, all of us, received as gift the mercy of God. Later in the Gospel of Matthew, Jesus tells his disciples, "freely you have received, freely give" (Matthew 10:8). The mercy God has shown us we are called upon to show each other. No more than it has been for God can mercy be for us a mechanical, measured, metered affair; the heart must be poured out. It is precisely in this context of the Sermon on the Mount that Jesus tells us, "Be perfect, therefore, as your heavenly Father is perfect" (Matthew 5:48).

It is a strange thing about us, the way we all long so much for love, understanding, trust and acceptance, yet so systematically reject all of them by our fear of being hurt. This is a great sign of sin, a lasting scar of evil in the tissues of our freedom. We long for others to trust us, yet cannot show them trust; we ache for understanding, yet are pleased to view others from prejudice; we crave tenderness, yet deal in cold currency. And we see all around us how lack of knowledge, closure, and distance generate destruction and alienation; how fear gives birth to fear. It is so hard for us to break out of this cycle. It is so hard for us to realize, not just in thought but in fact, that where there is no love we must put love in in order that we might draw love out (St. John of the Cross). It comes as a wonderful and somewhat overwhelming shock when we finally do risk our hearts in trust and discover we are trusted in return, when we show mercy and receive mercy back.

Of ourselves, our fear is so great we cannot do it. But our God has not only shown us what mercy is, he has given it to us in the gift of His Spirit (Romans 4:1–5). We who deserved nothing have been given all things by gift. The more we realize this, the more we will be able to entrust ourselves to each other in the gift of mercy, the more we will be able to take with each other the risk God has first taken with each of us.

Luke Timothy Johnson

Prayer for the Reader

There are times, Father, when I have to get away from everyone and be alone with You. Not to talk or to pray. Just to be—silently. Just to become astonished by Your presence. To feel Your nearness putting all the bits and pieces of me together again. You don't say a word, either—and yet I am healed. Isn't it amazing how much we seem to learn about each other as we share these quiet moments?

WHEN YOU'RE ENVIOUS

"You crave for something and don't get it; you are murderously jealous of what others have got and which you can't possess yourself."

(James 3:16, Phillips)

It's an uncomfortable sensation, an uneasy prickle you can't quite locate, a swift tensing of your body, and then—some thoughts you wish you'd never had. Maybe it happened during a conversation with a friend who was sharing good news about her life. All of a sudden the words started forming in your mind: "Why *her*? Why can't something like that happen to *me*?"

Your envy is showing

And you're ashamed of yourself. You thank God for helping you keep the words to yourself. Nevertheless—you thought them. You resented your friend for a moment; maybe even longer.

Why?

Because your friend's life seemed better than yours?

Because your friend seemed to be getting all the breaks—and you weren't getting any?

Because you think God may love your friend more than He loves you?

Silly, aren't they?

No. Not at all.

These are human feelings. Not our best feelings, but part of the way we're made. Being a Christian doesn't mean we won't be envious. It means we have to deal with the emotion.

> It is not a case of having a life with no difficulties, but of having the strength to surmount them.
>
> *Paul Tournier*

I know—you'd rather tell yourself you were wrong to feel that way, and promise yourself it will never happen again. Do that, and you'll end up like Saul, jealous enough to kill and telling yourself you're absolutely justified.

105

Do that, and you're Adam and Eve, believing the Devil when he tells you God isn't giving you enough of the good things in life. And, speaking of the Devil, wherever you find envy, you'll find his label on it. Envy is one of his specialties.

An odd thing about envy is that it usually shows up where love is. Or has been. Saul and David, Adam and Eve and God, Joseph and his brothers, the disciples jockeying for first place in heaven, Paul and the Corinthians—you and your friend with the good breaks. All of them in loving relationships until one person decided that the love wasn't evenly distributed—that one person was getting something the other deserved—that maybe God was playing favorites.

Now we're getting somewhere.

Notice that we usually aren't envious of someone we don't really like. Could it be that in some secret part of ourselves we feel that God doesn't like that person, either? And so, even if something wonderful happens to the person we don't like, we aren't threatened by it. His good fortune doesn't seem to have anything to do with his favor in God's eyes. It's just an accident. Those things happen.

But—someone we like, or admire, or love, that's different. Surely God finds that person lovable, too. More lovable than we are? Possibly. No, that couldn't be! God loves all of us equally.

Except that when I'm down and you're up, when my life is in a shambles and yours is mending, it's hard for me to believe that God loves me as much as He loves you. And, although I'm ashamed to admit it, I *am* threatened by your blessings when mine seem too few.

Why?

Because, like many Christians, I still measure God's love by visible proofs of it. Because, while I may not really believe that the more God loves me, the richer He's going to make me, I am inwardly shaken when a friend prospers and I don't. I become the Prodigal's brother, chafing at his father's embrace of the son who did everything wrong. I become a child, pouting: *I've been good—Why aren't you giving me a big party? Don't you love me anymore?*

That is envy. It preys on the spiritual child in us.

Not that there is anything wrong, or bad, about the spiritual child in us. There isn't. But, like children everywhere, this part of ourselves is very dependent upon external expressions of love: smiles, a pat on the head, words of praise, gifts. The child, who needs love even more than it can give love, is very sensitive to slights, real and imagined. Like all children, who depend upon their parents' love for existence, the spiritual child in us is terrified at the slightest indication that love might be withdrawn. What an ideal environment for the growth and development of envy!

I don't know about you, but I find that the child in me is perfectly happy with my own life when all is going well. That's when a friend—any friend, all friends—can prosper, succeed, be promoted, acknowledged with all kinds of gold medals, and I can share that friend's happiness. My child isn't the least bit threatened. It's only when *I* am having problems, that I can't handle another person's solutions very well. I feel left out, neglected. *Unloved.* My inner child hurts, and I don't know how to make the hurt go away.

Envy is a sin, there's no denying it. But we can't put a label on it and stop there. Envy won't go away by itself.

When I was a little girl and showed signs of being envious of someone, my elders always told me that I was foolish to think anyone's life was better than mine. If I really knew the other person, I was told, I might find out that he or she had every reason to be miserable. Never mind if the person appeared happy. *You never could tell!*

That kind of advice scared me. Did it mean that if I envied somebody, that person was going to end up unhappy? The truth of the matter usually was that the better I knew the persons I envied, the more enviable their lives appeared to be. Some people's grass really is greener most of the time.

But that is an adult realization, and it doesn't help the spiritual child in us when it feels threatened by a loss of love. And that is what envy is: a fear that we are not cherished, cared for, protected, nourished.

And therein lies an answer to the problem. This child in us needs our attention, our comfort, our assurance of God's love. And it needs that attention right in the midst of its envy.

Of course, it may be that you or I should change something in our lives, but I think it is much more realistic and important to change something in ourselves. It may be that the parasites which are eating away inside us, depriving us of the deeper joys and satisfactions of life, should become the object of our attention.

John Powell

I have to deal with envy every time I am involved in a typical family scene. It doesn't have to be anything special—just a simple family meal with everyone gathered around. Or a time of crisis when a family closes ranks in support of each other. The sight of a family cheerfully sharing the chores in a laundromat can bring tears of envy to my eyes. I am particularly vulnerable to family living because I missed so much of it. Yet because I do not have a family around me, I am often invited to share the activities of other families.

I can't tell you how many invitations I turned down over several years because I knew how envious I would be if I accepted. I also made a point of spending holidays alone or out of town (also alone). Consequently, I became more and more aware of the fact that I didn't have a family around me. I felt quite sorry for myself, too. Poor me. Lucky others!

Then, one Christmas season when I was planning my annual excuse to get out of all those invitations (and I can't believe how patient my friends were to keep extending them), I ran into a problem. It was going to be especially hard that year because I couldn't afford to go away. In fact, I was very short of money generally and not too optimistic about my future. My spirits couldn't have been lower, and I was throwing the door wide open to resentment toward anyone who seemed to be more fortunate than I was. I decided I wouldn't even have a Christmas tree that year—and I always used to have one, come what might. I wouldn't decorate my house or hang a wreath on the door. Actually I was sulking.

Almost every day I drove past a corner where Christmas trees were stacked in rows. There were trees of all sizes, but one in particular, a small fat one near the curb, kept catching my eye. And I kept turning my head away. No, I would not have a tree that year! I didn't have enough money. Poor me. Nobody cared what happened to me. Especially God.

But that tree stayed near the curb where I could see it. A lot of the other trees were sold, but it seemed that nobody wanted such a small one that year. What a shame. It had such a beautiful shape. I could put it on a table near the window, and at night, when the lights were on, people passing by could see it. I always liked the merry sight of a tree in a window at night.

It was two days before Christmas and I was driving past the corner again. This time I slowed down to get a better look and, sure enough, there it was. A very merry tree, indeed! I pulled over to the curb, parked my car and got out, hurrying to buy that tree before I could say no to myself—that is, if the price was right. The price was perfect; the tree seller was clearly glad to get rid of something no one else wanted.

I can't describe the excitement that was building up in me as I took the tree home and carried it into the house. I felt like a happy child. As I rummaged through the attic for my favorite ornaments, I began to sing Christmas carols out loud.

By the time I decorated the tree, it was dark. I turned on the lights and sat on the floor marveling at their sparkle. Then I realized that I didn't feel the least bit lonely. Or neglected. Or not loved. I felt, in fact, most generously cared for by a God who was especially close to me in those moments. He was sharing my frugalities, rejoicing in my small delights. We were going to spend Christmas together, He and I, and all the days thereafter, the good ones and the lean ones. I was going to worry about what I could do to make ends meet, and He was going to worry right along with me. Together we would explore ways to survive. My world was not nearly as dark as it had seemed when I thought I was alone. Something sparkled in it.

I knew what I wanted to do—and that was to be with people. With my family. For I realized that I did have a family after all. My friends, those who wanted me to be a part of their lives, they were my family and I was theirs. We needed to share each other's loaf and two fishes as well as each other's banquets, because what we really were sharing was our regard for each other.

I went to the phone and called the members of my family. "Come and see my wonderful little tree!" I said. "Somebody sent me a fruitcake and I'll make some eggnog. Bring anything else you like."

It was short notice for a gathering, but it didn't seem to matter. My house was filled that evening—with friends, with family, with caring.

So what was envy doing in a place like that? It wasn't. It was gone.

Prayer for the Reader

It will happen again, Lord. When I'm not looking, envy will slip into my life, and I will pull away from someone I have loved. I'm not trying to make excuses, but sometimes life gets pretty scary. And when that happens, I do feel like a child. Everyone else seems big and competent and secure, while I seem small, helpless, insignificant. But You understand children. Suffer me to come to You even when I am not particularly lovable. Help me to clear the envy from my eyes by granting me Your vision.

WHEN YOU NEED MONEY

"Yes, ask anything, using my name...."

(John 14:14, Living Bible)

Face it. It can happen to anyone. No matter how carefully we budget, or how hard we try to make the dollars stretch, sometimes there isn't enough money left to meet our needs. Sometimes, especially in these difficult economic times, the money we counted on simply isn't there. Then what?

It's a painful situation. While money is vital to survival, it is also a subject that arouses uncomfortable emotions. The first is fear; the prospect of running out of money is chilling. But there is also the matter of shame. Most of us were brought up to think that there is something wrong—disgraceful, almost—about needing money. After all, if we live within our means, if we don't buy a lot of material things we really don't need, then we shouldn't ever need money. Isn't that true? It's nice to think so, but life isn't always so predictable. Businesses fail, jobs disappear, illness strikes, to name some of the more common disasters that can wipe out our financial resources. But on the plus side, we may come across a good opportunity that requires more money than we have available. The couple with two young children, squeezed into a city apartment and no back yard, may not yet have a down payment for the little house on a tree-lined street that just came on the market. The retired couple who would like to move into a retirement community, where housekeeping is provided and all their rooms are on one floor, may not be able to afford it even if they sell their paid-up house. A young graduate from law school needs money to open an office. A steel worker laid off for ten months wants to go back to school for training in another field. A minister whose work load is especially heavy, and has been for years, could use a modest vacation. A young mother, very devoted to her children, wishes she could afford a babysitter—just once in a while. Her husband wishes he could treat his wife to dinner in a restaurant—nothing lavish—and he can't remember the last time he did.

We live in a world that is full of material needs. At this moment I can think of a handicapped man who needs a job to restore his self-respect and sense of usefulness; a mother with a brain-damaged child who needs a means of transportation to get her daughter to the nearest special school; a Southeast Asian refugee family that needs housing, food, and a tutor to help them with their new language. And there are many more. Yet in so many of these instances we hear the same words: "I just can't ask God for material things."

...Yet there is that word *bread*, and what could be more down-to-earth than that? Surely, if Jesus meant for us to communicate with God only about spiritual matters, He would have used a different word. Bread is the simplest kind of food, the very staple of life from the beginning of recorded time. It has literally been the nutritional mainstay of civilization. And it is nourishment we need regularly, day by day, as Jesus also acknowledged by calling it "our *daily* bread."

Colleen Townsend Evans

I don't think I am unusual in having been brought up to think it is wrong to want more money than I have available to me. And while that is a good way to avoid getting into extravagant habits, it also prevents us from putting money in its proper perspective. Money is a means to an end, and that end is an important matter.

I can remember very well the uncomfortable feeling that came over me when I was in high school and my teachers began encouraging me to think about going on to college. Those weren't the days when everybody went to college, and certainly not every girl, so it came as a bit of a shock to my parents when I told them what my teachers were saying. Naturally, my parents were pleased with my academic achievements, but the cost of a college career was something they had never included in their plans for the future. Nevertheless they said they would think about it. I did more than that. I began to plan on going to college. I had been brought up to be thankful for the necessities in life and never to ask for luxuries, but I couldn't see how that ruled out a college education. To me, once I considered the possibility that I might be college material, the attempt had to be made. Learning, I was beginning to realize, was food for some essential part of me I was just beginning to discover.

I applied to several colleges, all of them within commuting distance to eliminate the cost of boarding. I took and passed the entrance exams. I waited.

I was accepted! It was the college I most earnestly wanted to attend, but the one I was certain would turn me down because its standards were so high. And then my parents sat me down at our kitchen table and, holding back tears, explained to me why they couldn't afford to pay my tuition.

I couldn't cry, not in front of them. They had done their best to help me. But later, in my room, I stuffed the corner of my pillow in my mouth so they wouldn't hear my sobs.

It had never occurred to me to ask God for help. After all, this was a matter of money, and money seemed too unclean a subject to discuss with God.

It took a few sleepless nights and some fidgety days for me to swallow my pride—yes, it was *pride!*—and ask God to help me find a way to get some of that crass green substance so that I could feed the hunger which He seemed to have given me. Maybe I was rationalizing; maybe not. All I remember is that, at the end of my increasingly frantic prayer, I said, "Lord, if You can't just *give* me the money, help me find a way to *earn* it! I'm willing to work!" I felt better about that.

The next day I began reading the help wanted ads in our community paper. I didn't expect to find anything because I was still in school most of the day and could work only a few hours. Who would want me?

A dentist.

There it was, in so many words. A local dentist needed someone to develop his films and type letters for a few hours a week. I knew nothing about negative processing, but I applied. The processing, it turned out, was a simple matter which I could learn quickly. I already knew how to type. And my availability after school meshed perfectly with the dentist's schedule. I had a job! Come summer, when I could put in more hours, I had a better job, with more pay. It was a beginning.

My parents were troubled by my persistence. They were afraid I would be hurt—badly—at the very last moment. But by then I was over my shyness with God. Money was the means to an education which would enable me to develop the talents He had given me, and I felt comfortable about asking for help.

I got help. Lots of it. My parents scraped together all kinds of extra pennies, and I managed to find part-time jobs throughout four years of college. At one particularly precarious time, I was awarded a small scholarship (in those days they were scarce) and a grant-in-aid which I could repay without interest after I had graduated and was earning a living.

For four years I commuted every school day by bus, ferry boat and a mile-long uphill walk through an unattractive part of New York City—and never, for one minute, felt deprived or in any way in want. Quite the contrary, I was exhilarated! I felt as if God and I were doing it together, which indeed we were. He was guiding me toward the person He wanted me to become, and money was simply the ticket I had to get punched along the way.

Again, I thought of myself as being among those early Christians who were with Christ. Surely, they had money shortages. And just as surely, they had to talk to him about their needs. Perhaps *needs* is the key word we should consider. Money itself is not a need; it must serve a need, or it is not worth mentioning. If the need is worth God's attention, then we can ask Him for help in getting the money to serve that need.

As I went through college I had to borrow some money to help pay the expenses; so when I started preaching, I was in debt.

I remember some of the letters the finance company wrote when I got behind on my car payments. They were fearful!

In those years we didn't have to have many clothes, but we had to buy some along the way. I remember an overcoat I bought for five dollars down and five dollars a month. I missed so many payments that by the time I finally made the last one, the coat was worn threadbare. We even bought our groceries on credit. My limited credit at the grocery store is one reason why I am so skinny today.

In those years it took every dollar I got to pay for something I had already eaten up or worn out. It worried me to be in debt. I don't remember asking God to let those debts be "forgiven," but I did pray many times asking God to show me how to make enough money to pay up everything.

We worked hard, the Lord helped us, and finally there came a day when all our debts were paid. There were no more mean letters about our payments being behind, and what money we had was clear and free. A great burden was lifted from my mind, and I felt new joy and happiness.

Charles L. Allen

We children certainly did not enjoy those Depression years, yet no tinge of fear about lack of money ever clouded our home. It never seemed even to have entered Mother's head that we were living through a period of poverty. She went through each difficult day of the depression as though she had some secret bank account to draw from when we were in need—and in a sense she did. But her real secret was an utterly confident inner attitude: always before her was a picture of a healthy, fulfilled family.

Though we did without many things, Mother always provided us with a feeling of well-being. One way she did this was the unique manner in which she contrived to give to others. Out of our meager pantry she would send a sick neighbor a supper tray of something delicious she had prepared—velvety smooth, boiled custard; feather-light, homemade rolls—served up on our best china and always with a dainty bouquet from our garden.

Catherine Marshall

Prayer for the Reader

Make me bold, Father. Help me to understand that my reluctance to ask You for help comes between us as much as any greed I might have. If my need is genuine, if it will enable me to serve You better, then let me share it with You now.

WHEN YOU HAVE TOO MUCH TO DO

"I will put upon you none other burden."

(Revelation 2:24, KJV)

It scared me. I had never experienced anything like it. Ever. I felt empty, hollow. I could perceive the world around me and everything in it, but my mind refused to put the pieces together. It refused to think, consider, or care. In fact, my lack of concern was what told me something was wrong. When I *can't* care about my work, about what is happening to my friends and family, then I *know* I'm in trouble.

> When we lose waking up in the morning as though each day was going to be full of adventure, joys, and dangers, and wake up instead to the alarm clock (as most of us must; and how lovely those rare nights when we look at the clock and don't have to set the alarm), and the daily grind, and mutter about TGIF, we lose the newborn quality of belief which is so lovely in the child.
>
> *Madeleine L'Engle*

I was worn out from caring, from doing, from *being*. I couldn't remember the last time I took a day off. My heart still wanted to pull me in six directions at once, but the rest of me just wouldn't go along. I never thought that would happen to me. Why did it?

I think God was sending me a message: STOP!

That's right. STOP! Right in the middle of everything. No, I hadn't finished what I was trying to do. And there wasn't anyone who could take over for me. If the world was going to fall in on me, there wasn't anything I could do about it.

My fear brought me very close to God. Or, rather, it brought Him close to me. And I leaned on Him. I had no choice. I was simply out of giving.

I took the telephone off the hook. I covered my typewriter. I didn't have the energy to put my desk in order. My house was a mess. The laundry wasn't done. I hadn't even thought about dinner. I wasn't hungry. I settled my puppy and cat and then I settled myself in bed. It felt so strange lying there in the daylight. I've never been one to take a nap.

You and I must open ourselves to the question: What is life for? We should get right down into the fabric of our daily lives. What am I doing? Is my life a series of deadlines...meetings ...clearing my desk...answering phones...moving from one crisis to the next? Do I look forward to the stretch of life that is ahead of me? To next week? To the coming year? Is mine a hand-to-mouth existence? Is it a matter of "getting by"? When I wake up in the morning, is my first reaction: "Good morning, God!" or "Good God, morning!"? Am I in a survival context? Do I feel trapped? Am I just hanging on? Am I asking: How much longer can I take this?

John Powell

We are in too big a hurry, and we run by far more than we catch up with. The Bible tells us to "Be still, and know that I am God" (Psalm 46:10). Beauty doesn't shout. Loveliness is quiet. Our finest moods are not clamorous. The familiar appeals of the Divine are always in calm tones, a still, small voice.

Charles L. Allen

I was too tired to sleep and I lay staring up at the ceiling, its whiteness a welcome blank. I could feel my mind resting, refusing all thoughts that tried to intrude on it. The emptiness in me became so great that I began to cry. I was afraid I would never have any energy again. Could such a thing happen, Lord?

His answer came slowly, over several days. The first thing I felt was a sense of peacefulness filling that terrible emptiness. It was all right to be helpless, it seemed to assure me. It was all right to run out of steam after using too much of it for too long. I was perfectly normal. I remember smiling about that as I dropped off into sleep. In broad daylight.

When I woke up it was dark. My cat was curled up next to me and my puppy's cold nose brushed my cheek lightly. I felt cared for. The burden had been lifted.

I had not fully recovered. But I knew I would. In time. I put myself entirely in God's hands. *If you want me to rest, then I'll find a way*, I promised. *But, Lord, I do want my energy back!*

He gave it back a little each day. And one morning I awoke with the zest that was so typical of me. The first thing I did with it was thank God. I'm afraid I was awfully loud about it, but that's how grateful I felt.

I know now that I am as human as you are. Or as anyone else is. I have been blessed with a lot of energy, with marvelous health, and I like to get things done. But I do have my limits, and I ignored that part of my human condition for too long. Finally God had to step in and do something about it. I won't allow that to become necessary again. I know how to rest now—right in the middle of everything. And I discovered something else: the world doesn't fall in on my head when I take a break. It keeps right on turning—because that's His job, not mine.

Prayer for the Reader

No, Lord, I don't want to stop what I'm doing. Nobody gave me these burdens—I put them on myself. I like getting things done. I want to help people. Don't ask me to change—You're the One Who made me this way. But I'm sure You gave me more sense than I've been using. If I'm so good at doing things, then I ought to be able to learn how to pace myself. Thanks for the warning.

FALLING IN LOVE

"I am overcome by one glance of your eyes... How sweet is your love, my darling."

(Song of Solomon 4:9–10, Living Bible)

It's everything everyone said it would be. Only more.

It's physical: wobbly knees, a sudden plummeting sensation from head to toe, a constant smile—which some people call "silly," but you couldn't care less—a forgetfulness, an inertia that leaves you sitting, staring into space, a tremendous appetite, or none at all.

It's mental: you aren't in the here and now. You're in a beautiful fantasy land inhabited by only the two of you. Everything is perfect. Even the colors are muted, soft, rainbow-like. No discordant sounds; harps playing in the background. You know you have discovered the meaning of happiness, and you know it will never end. Aren't you lucky!

It's spiritual, you're sure of that: this is the person in all the world who was meant specifically for you. And you for that person. It must be God who is bringing you together—it must be, or why would you be feeling this way?

Actually, there are a million reasons why, but the most important one is that right now you are ready to fall in love. And the only thing God has to do with it is that He created in each of you this capacity to give yourself to another.

Which is fine. Except that there is a crucial difference between giving and abandoning one's self. God never meant you to surrender what He created in you. It isn't even yours to give away because it belongs to Him. He means for you to share it. He means for you to experience a willingness to give to another what is wonderful and good within you; He means for you to learn, through another human being, that you are worth loving—so that you will have a clearer understanding of His spiritual devotion to you; He means for you to put the well-being of another ahead of your own. He does not mean for you to dispose of yourself.

It is that all which can never be asked, fairly, by any human being, not mother, not father, not lover, not child. In our human

120

relationships we are protected by the knowledge that no one can demand all of us, that we may and should keep something back, and that in doing so we are justified. Only one power in the universe has the right to ask that all of us; that power alone can ask it, and ask it fairly; and we wish in some part of ourselves that this all would not be asked.

Emilie Griffin

Giving the gift of myself in love leaves me with a deep and lasting satisfaction of having done something good with my life. . . I am left with a sense of having used well the gifts which God has invested in me.

John Powell

If you have love, you can give it. If you don't have it, you don't have it to give. Actually it's not really even a matter of giving, is it? It's a matter of sharing. Whatever I have I can share with you. I don't lose it because I still have it. For example, I could teach every reader everything I know. I would still know everything I know. It is possible for me—and not unreasonable—to love everyone with equal intensity and still have all the love energy I have ever had.

Leo Buscaglia

"He's the most wonderful thing that ever happened to me!"
"She changed my whole life!"
"She's everything I need!"
"I realize now that I never really loved anyone until him!"
"I'd go anywhere just to be with him!"
With one exception, these are not the remarks of a teenager. One was spoken by a woman in her sixties, a widow, about a man in his seventies,

a widower she was about to marry after knowing him a few weeks. One was spoken by a man whose first marriage started out ecstatically and ended in divorce. Falling in love is something that can happen to any of us at any point in life. And while it can lead to real love, it is not the same as love.

Like any other swift descent, falling in love has its hazards. It takes our breath away and interferes with our vision.

> . . . Let's establish that love and compatibility are two very different things. Simply because we are profoundly attracted to people and have passionate feelings of love doesn't mean for a moment that we should *marry* them. Falling in love is easy. Some people can do it at the drop of a hat. But such people may have to fall in and out of love several times before they discover others with whom they could happily spend the rest of their lives.
>
> There are also people with whom we are compatible, but whom we don't love. What we need is someone who is both.
>
> . . . We have been programmed by our culture, by the depiction of love on the screen, and by popular songs to think of love as the major solution to all our problems. It is the Holy Grail which, if recovered, will bring ultimate happiness.
>
> This is a disastrous path, for we are expecting romance to give us something that only religion is designed to offer. When we begin to worship romantic love, it collapses under the weight.
>
> *Alan Loy McGinnis*

Is it wrong, then, to fall in love? Should we run the other way when it happens? No.

We have to assume that since God gave us the capacity to feel things deeply, our emotions have some worthwhile purpose. And this is especially true of romantic love. Whatever impels us to leave the family and surroundings we know, and venture into a totally unfamiliar partnership with another, has to be powerful. There are cords, however good, that must be broken or at least loosened so that we can begin a new and adult life. Falling in love is the most effective cord-breaker of all time. It gives us the courage to give up the only security we have ever known; it convinces us that the preferences, thoughts, values and behavior of another will make our own life richer; it promises us that we, and we alone, can meet the life needs of the other.

But can we trust these assurances? Absolutely not. At this point we are willing to believe anything that tells us that what we are feeling really is love. What we need at this critical moment is help from a Friend, and ironically this is the one part of life we often insist on determining by ourselves. After all, we decide, what would Jesus Christ know about falling in love?

Everything.

Because He fell in love with us. Because that powerful emotion enabled Him to wrench Himself away from the security of His home with His Father and to give Himself totally over to our well-being. And yet never to give away the essence of God that was in Him. Yes, He knows all about falling in love, and unless we can experience this sensation in the way He did, then it is not real love we are talking about.

> Agape love enriches our family ties, our national ties, our ethnic ties. Agape love makes us more sensitive to the wonder of the world around us and to the various people who enter our lives. Agape love even makes us more intimate with those in the very inner circle. Agape makes us better lovers. Its fundamental acceptance of the person next to us enriches eros. It completes beauty and intimacy.
>
> *Earl F. Palmer*

The falling part of love may be bliss, in a way, but love itself certainly isn't. Much of the time love is very painful.

> Are you capable of forgiving and accepting in love a world which has disappointed you by not being perfect, a world in which there is so much unfairness and cruelty, disease and

crime, earthquake and accident? Can you forgive its imperfections and love it because it is capable of containing great beauty and goodness, and because it is the only world we have?

Are you capable of forgiving and loving the people around you, even if they have hurt you and let you down by not being perfect? Can you forgive them and love them, because there aren't any perfect people around, and because the penalty for not being able to love imperfect people is condemning oneself to loneliness?

Harold S. Kushner

This person you feel so deeply about—ask yourself if you can take his rejection, his misunderstanding of your devotion to him, his insistence that he will stand by you in your time of need and his excuses when he doesn't. Can you put up with her selfishness, her foolishness, her obsessive need to be with you every waking moment without regard for your fatigue? Can you tolerate the endless questions, the sulking when you won't change the course of your life, the resentment of your closeness with your friends, your family, with God? Can you stand not being appreciated?

And still love this other person?

Jesus can. He could. He does. This is love. Falling or standing still, this is love. Is it what *you* feel? Is it what the other feels for you? This is a time to ask questions. The answers may not be quick in coming.

Prayer for the Reader

Thank you, Lord, for this ability to care for another. I am, in fact, a little giddy from caring, and I can't trust my sense of direction. I'll feel much better about it if You will come along with me on this journey.

INVESTING YOUR TALENT

"And some of the parts that seem weakest and least important are really the most necessary."

(I Corinthians 12:22, Living Bible)

"And what do *you* do?"

It's a tricky question to answer. But not if you have a talent. You can make sense out of computers. You can sing. You can paint, and in fact some of your paintings have been sold, so you *must* be good. You can find out what's wrong with people physically and emotionally. You can make lots of money. You used to be a dancer and now you teach. Your talent is your label. It's what you can tell people you are.

But—suppose you don't think you have a talent? How can you describe yourself? I mean, suppose you can brighten up the dark parts of a room with a touch of color. Or bring a garden to life in a window box high up over a city street. Or you're a person who remembers the important days in other people's lives and you do something about them. Maybe you know what a sick person needs without asking. Or you write newsy letters to friends you don't get to see often. What do you call these things?

They are talents. Every bit as much as an ability that enables someone to rise in the fields of business, art, science or entertainment. Your talents may not make money for you, but they certainly accomplish what a talent is meant to do—which is, to carry out God's work in the world.

A sad fact which nevertheless needs to be faced is that a deeply committed Christian who wants to write stories or paint pictures or compose music to the glory of God simply may not have been given the talent, the gift, which a non-Christian, or even an atheist, may have in abundance. God is no respecter of persons, and this is something we are reluctant to face. . . .

Often we forget that He has a special gift for each one of us, because we tend to weigh and measure such gifts with the coin of the world's market place. The widow's mite was worth more than all the rich men's gold because it represented the focus of her life. Her poverty was rich because all she had belonged to the living Lord. Some unheard-of Elizabethan woman who led a life of selfless love may well be brought before the throne of God ahead of Shakespeare, for such a person may be a greater force for good than someone on whom God's blessings seem to have been dropped more generously.

Madeleine L'Engle

The marvelous richness of human experience would lose something of rewarding joy if there were no limitations to overcome. The hilltop hour would not be half so wonderful if there were no dark valleys to traverse.

I have never believed that my limitations were in any sense punishments or accidents. If I had held such a view, I could never have exerted the strength to overcome them.

Helen Keller

So if you are using your talent to make a part of the world a little better for the rest of us, then you're investing it.

That's what *you* do!

Prayer for the Reader

It's not the big-name talents I'm concerned about, Jesus. I'm under a lot of pressure to make the most of them. We all have to be very clever to make a living these days. But I may be overlooking the other talents you gave me, the ones that bring me close to people. Kindness, for instance. Understanding. A joy in giving. A sensitivity to unspoken need. Make me aware of these gifts, dear Lord. I think they may be what I need to go with You in Your world.

WHEN EVERYTHING SEEMS TO BE GOING WRONG

"We are perplexed because we don't know why things happen as they do, but we don't give up and quit."

(II Corinthians 4:8, Living Bible)

Everywhere you turn, you meet problems, obstacles, difficulties. Large ones, small ones, all sizes. None of your dreams is coming true. You can deal with disappointment, but not so much of it all at once.

You don't want to say it, but you can't help it—Why? you ask. Why is this happening to you?

Most of us, unfortunately, feel like a floating boat at the mercy of the winds and waves. We have no ballast when the winds rage and the waves churn. We say things like: "He made me so mad." "You really get to me." "Her remark embarrassed me terribly." "This weather really depresses me." "This job really bores me." "The very sight of him saddens me.". . . And, like all men we are content to blame others, circumstances, and bad luck. The fully human person, as Shakespeare puts it in *Julius Caesar*, knows that: "The fault, dear Brutus, is not with our stars, but with ourselves. . . ." We can rise above the dust of daily battle that chokes and blinds so many of us; and this is precisely what is asked of us in the process of growth as a person.

John Powell

I experienced the most intense misery I've ever known. Life went gray. Nor was it all psychological or spiritual. Events in the exterior world began going against me. Things like: a major Hollywood studio purchased my novel *Christy*, then decided not to produce it. The fiction manuscript on which I began working was presenting problems so great that I began to see that after pouring myself into it for three years, I was going to have to suspend work on it. An almost wild succession of small, vexing personal inconveniences came on in waves: the dish-

127

washer went out; the bathroom plumbing went awry; a truck driver backed into our mailbox and demolished it; the lawn developed cinch bugs; the car kept stopping cold on us. . . .

If we don't accept the circumstances God's permissive will has allowed and ask, "Lord, what is Your will for me in the midst of these circumstances?," then He permits the difficulties to heap up. For most of us that's the only way He can get our attention.

In my misery He had my attention all right. Obviously I was meant to turn off my grumbling and wait upon Him. I was to listen and to learn.

Catherine Marshall

You tell yourself your problems won't last forever. You know you still have some blessings you can count. But—you're tired of looking for solutions. You're tired of being brave. Yet you don't want to complain.

Do we carry about with us a sense of God? Do we carry the thought of Him with us wherever we go? If not, we have missed the greatest part of life. Do we have the feeling and conviction of God's abiding presence wherever we go?

Henry Drummond

Of course, He cares. When you hurt, He hurts. Tell Him. It's all right to cry on His shoulder. Tears don't mean you're weak. They mean you feel. And He made you that way.

He meets life as a man, calls on no power that is not at your disposal and mine. He is so like me that I feel I might put my hand on His shoulder and say, "Brother man."

E. Stanley Jones

Have you ever stopped to think how foolish we are to act as though God knew *nothing* of our conflicts, our inner battles? As though we and we alone knew? . . .There is only danger in not discussing *everything*—all our conflicts and our stubbornness and rebellions with God. There is only danger in not talking it all over with him—just as it is. If we are unwilling to let go of a thing or a person or an attitude, it is better to be honest with God and ask him to show us how to let go. Or to make us willing to be willing. He knows anyway.

Eugenia Price

Remember when everything was going well? Or *do* you remember? It's funny, but when the waters of life are smooth and untroubled, we don't seem to notice. We don't stop and say, "Thank you, Lord, for these good moments." Later we look back on them with longing. Will we ever know them again? Of course, we will. And perhaps we'll take time to stop and savor them.

I'm glad the writers of the Scriptures left those giants of faith with their fears, loneliness, and frustrations plainly visible. It helps me to know, in a *real* way, that my perfect little world, the one I want to see so badly, is rarely going to be perfect. In fact, no number of spiritual rationalizations or tired cliches can make it so. . . .I *do* have brief moments of glorious perfection. . . .There are times when I *know* I've done very well, or God allows a relationship to be healed, and the victory leaves me heady with joy. At these times, I experience a marvelous wholeness in Christ. But, at the same time, I must not be blind about the way sin and Satan have crippled our world and our thinking. For life in the real world has a way of shattering the desired perfection we long to possess on a regular basis.

Joyce Landorf

No, your troubles won't last forever—but what are you going to do in the meantime? Is it possible—just maybe—that you can become a more loving person? Why not? You possess the gift of resurrection!

When my strength is depleted...when I am weary, the Lord has a much better tool for empathetic, sensitive communication. The barriers are down. When I know I can do nothing by myself, my poverty becomes a channel of his power....It's taken me a long time to learn that the lower my resistances are and the less self-consciousness I have, the more the Word of God comes through. There is less of the club of judgment and more of a cross of grace....I need to hear what I am saying more than the listeners; the result is that they hear what I may have blocked from them before.

What about you? Are you feeling weak or fearful right now? Thank God!...Embrace the troubled moment; make it a friend.

Lloyd John Ogilvie

Do you realize then, what a miracle you are experiencing? In the midst of your heartbreak, your anxiety, your despair, you are being recreated. You are finding qualities of your being that you never knew existed. Don't forget them when the problems are solved. And don't dwell on them when the moments are good—there is no need for that. But the next time you are overwhelmed by misfortunes, you won't have to ask, Why? You'll know you are approaching a time of discovery.

I will greet this day with love in my heart.

And how will I do this? Henceforth will I look on all things with love and I will be born again. I will love the sun for it warms my bones; yet I will love the rain for it cleanses my spirit. I will love the light for it shows me the way; yet I will love the darkness for it shows me the stars. I will welcome happiness for it enlarges my heart; yet I will endure sadness for it opens my soul. I will acknowledge rewards for they are my due; yet I will welcome obstacles for they are my challenge.

Og Mandino

Prayer for the Reader

Father, let the times of testing stretch me—but not so far that I lose touch with You. While I am in this needy condition, lead me into a deeper understanding of others' feelings. Let me not forget the sting of tears so that when I see them in another's eyes I will tend the wound that caused them.

WHEN YOU AREN'T APPRECIATED

"I receive not honour from men."

(John 5:41, KJV)

Don't put up with it.

If you can't ever seem to do enough, if you aren't being paid what you are worth, if the credit for your achievements is given to someone else, or none is given at all—if who you are and what you do are taken for granted, don't swallow hard and put up with it. Go to those who will appreciate you.

Not out of spite. Not out of anger or because you are defeated. But out of sensibility. You have an obligation to God and to yourself: God has made you what you are so that He can work through you. You are the channel for His Power. But God can't do anything with you or through you if you aren't appreciated.

Many men feel as insecure and worthless as do similarly troubled members of the gentle sex. In fact, low self-esteem is a threat to the entire human family, affecting children, adolescents, the elderly, all socioeconomic levels of society, and each race and ethnic culture. It can engulf anyone who feels disrespected in the eyes of other people. At least 90 percent of our self-concept is built from what we think others think about us. I can hardly respect myself, obviously, if the rest of the world seems to believe that I am dumb or ugly or lazy or boring or uncreative or undesirable.

A very old proverb reads, "No one can stand the awful knowledge that he is not needed." What wisdom is recorded in that phrase! It is not uncommon for a man to develop major illnesses within a few months following his retirement. Just knowing that his job is finished often accelerates the process of deterioration. A well-known physician-author stated recently that a man who believes he has no further worth or purpose in living will be dead in eighteen months. Likewise, the most rebellious, hostile teenagers are usually those who are bitterly disappointed with whom they are and what they are becoming.

James Dobson

Somebody has got to come up occasionally and pat us on the shoulder and say, "Wow! That's good. I really like that." It would be a miracle if we could let people know what was right rather than always pointing out what is wrong.

Leo Buscaglia

We're not talking about praise. You are not asking for a medal of commendation. Your self-esteem, bruised as it may be, does not *require* the acclamation of others. But you do need recognition for the person that you are. Your presence in the world, and among those close to you, needs to be acknowledged. A head must nod—yes, you are here, and you are welcome. It's the difference between being called by your name or beckoned with a wave of a hand. Appreciation identifies us as one of God's children.

And if we aren't identified, we become unproductive:

When Jesus. . .came into his own country. . . .he taught the people in their own synagogue, till in their amazement they said: "Where does this man get this wisdom and these powers? He's only the carpenter's Son. Isn't Mary his mother, and aren't James, Joseph, Simon and Judas his brothers? And aren't all his sisters living here with us? Where did he get all this?" And they were deeply offended with him.

But Jesus said to them, "No prophet goes unhonored except in his own country and in his own home!"

And he performed very few miracles there because of the lack of faith.

(Matthew 13: 53–58, Phillips)

When you aren't appreciated, it's because someone doesn't have faith in you or in your abilities, even though you may have demonstrated them. And it's not your fault. Some people just don't have the capacity to believe.

The important thing is for you to keep faith in yourself, to remember that God created you and you will always have His appreciation. So do what

133

Jesus did when He wasn't appreciated. He went on from there. You need a success experience. Allow God to lead you to it.

You are, before the Lord, a very important person. This is not just good psychology; this is good, sound, Biblical doctrine. God sent His Son because He loves you. Romans 8:29 says that God is conforming us, since He is working on us as His unique vessels. . . .

Picture yourself as a priceless diamond in the rough. God works away on you, buffeting and polishing, grinding and filing. The diamond is being shaped and prepared for the perfect plan He has for you. But at times the process is definitely irritating. *The one who frequently feels inferior is the one who concentrates on the part that isn't finished rather than on the part that is being completed or has already been shaped.* God is working on you—He just isn't finished. Remember the key word: *persevere!*

Charles Swindoll

Prayer for the Reader

Make me aware, Father, of the others in my life. Help me to look at them in newness and in faith. Give me the vision to discover You in each person. And give me a voice to tell them, in so many words, how much they mean to me.

WHEN YOU'RE ILL

"And whatever their illness and pain...he healed them all."

(Matthew 4:24, Living Bible)

When we're very young, we almost enjoy being sick. As long as it isn't serious. We become, for a while, the most important persons in the world, the center of everyone's attention. Mothers persuade us to eat our favorite foods. Fathers take time to read us stories and press a hand across our forehead before they say good night; everyone definitely becomes more affectionate. Brothers and sisters willingly surrender their fondest possessions; all we have to do is look, longingly. All blame, all wrongs, all sins, are wiped out. Our slate is clean. Only we get well.

We almost don't want to get well. Except that being sick gets boring. It still does. Especially when we aren't very young.

Illness can also be frightening to an adult. It comes uninvited, pushing all our priorities aside, stranding us in our bed, in our room, or, worse, in a hospital. The rhythmic pattern of every day is totally disrupted, and we are adrift in a sea of uncertainty.

This time there is no fussing over us. No one has the time. We, who have stopped whirling and dashing about, now become distressingly aware of how busy everyone else is. Of course, we are loved. We are cause for concern. But there are no dishes of ice cream to tempt our appetites, no trays of sweet tea and buttered toast—unless we can manage to make them for ourselves.

There are, however, worries. Who will do our work for us? Who will look after our family, fill in for us in our job? Who will pay the bills for our recovery? Illness isn't child's play anymore, is it?

It was awful! One day I was fine, trying to do six things at once, as usual—and then, that fatigue. It would go away, I told myself. A good night's sleep would fix everything.

The next day I was in the hospital undergoing all kinds of tests. That in itself was frightening.

They told me I had hepatitis. If I behaved myself, if I followed doctor's orders to the letter, I might recover within a year.

I'm told that men are terrible patients, and now I know it's true. The diagnosis was like a prison sentence, and I treated my wife as if she were my jailer. I tried so hard to get well fast that I ended up in the hospital again, and that taught me a lesson. I would have to slow down, something I had never been able to do in my life.

Doing nothing was depressing. I lost my appetite. I didn't want to read. I didn't even want to talk to visitors. I felt as if my life were over.

Then a funny thing happened. I was lying in bed, staring out the window, when I saw my son coming down the street. It was too early for him to be out of school. Something must be wrong! And from the look of him, there certainly was. His head was down and there was no spring in his step.

I heard the door open and then close. Then footsteps on the stairs. But no Billy poking his head in the door with a "Hi, Dad." He went straight to his room. And I heard him sobbing. This is a boy who almost never cried.

I got up and went to his room. I knocked. I could tell he was pushing his face into the pillow so I wouldn't hear him crying.

"Billy?" I called softly. "Can I come in?"

"I guess," he said.

I'll never forget that day. If I hadn't been home recuperating, I wouldn't have been around when my son was going through a rough time. Billy's an athlete, a fine one. His dream is to qualify for an Olympics relay team, but that's a little way off in the future. Meanwhile he worked out every morning, trying to be the best and fastest runner there ever was. He knew that if he was good enough, he could get a scholarship to pay for a good part of his college expenses. And that day, the day he came home dragging his feet, he had just been told he didn't get the scholarship. Somebody else was better than he was.

Sure, he cried. I cried, too. And then we both began to realize that there was more to life than not getting what you wanted: Billy's scholarship and my recovery. The important thing is to try again.

136

I think that was the first time my son and I prayed with tears still wet on our faces. I know it was the first time we knelt together. We weren't trying to appear big and strong to each other then. We both knew we needed help. We weren't very strong at all, and we were very aware of the fact that Jesus Christ was bigger and stronger than the two of us put together.

Billy laced up his shoes and went out for a run. He wasn't exactly grinning, but at least his head was up.

And I? Well, I went back to my room, got into bed, and pulled a pad out of the nightstand drawer. I began making a list of books I wanted to read—*had* wanted to read for a long time and never got around to them. It was time for me to catch up on some of the things that had been happening in my profession. It was time for me to start making use of this time of recovery instead of just sitting around, getting stale.

But there was one book I wanted to read that I already had, and I reached for it. We always kept a Bible on the nightstand, but in all those weeks I had been a patient, I hadn't even opened it. I thought I knew everything it had to say—and what could it possibly say about being sick?

I knew what I was looking for, but I could only remember the beginning of the verse. There—I found it! "In everything give thanks; for this is the will of God in Christ Jesus for you" (I Thessalonians 5:18, NKJV).

Howard Hawkins

Illness can be a time of exquisite solitude—if we allow God to share it with us. When we are well and vigorous, we savor our own strength, but in the weakness that accompanies illness, we are suddenly aware of God's amazing vitality. It is He reaching out to us now, and if we are very still, we can feel His healing.

And so one interminable month dragged by after another.

On an especially low day Peter would often stand in the bedroom looking down at me propped up on the pillows, and turn prophet. "Cath'rine, someday you will look back with gratitude on these bleak days as some of the richest of your life." Then, seeing my incredulous inability to receive his words: "Besides, Cath'rine, you know perfectly well, *all* discouragement is of Satan."

I just wanted to throw a book at my Scottish prophet. Whereupon he would grin and pat my cheek and kiss me, turn on his heel and depart for the church office.

Yet looking back, I know that Peter was right. For me those two years in bed were a continuation in depth of the voyage of self-discovery and God-discovery begun in college.

The unforgettable truth of David's Psalm 23 came alive in my experience: "He *maketh* me to lie down in green pastures. . ." Thus sometimes using illness to get our full attention. For me this became a period of equipping—of spiritual preparation— for a tumultuous life of changes, of great, high moments to follow and plunging low points. From the vantage point of years, I can see now that my being forced to lie down in the green pastures beside very still waters indeed—the isolation of our bedroom—was a time of training. Day by day God was the Teacher and I, the pupil.

Catherine Marshall

But—suppose we don't recover? There is always that fear when we are ill. Are we being told the truth? No—we don't want to know the truth, not if it's bad!

The example of the newly blinded man is so concrete, I wish to use it as a type for all life-training. When he first loses his sight, he thinks there is nothing left for him but heartache and despair. He feels shut out from all that is human. Life to him is like the ashes on a cold hearth. The fire of ambition is quenched. The light of hope is gone out. The objects in which he once took delight seem to thrust out sharp edges at him as he gropes his way about. Even those who love him act unwittingly as an irritant to his feelings because he can no longer give them the support of his labour. Then comes some wise teacher and friend and assures him he can work with his hands and to a considerable degree train his hearing to take the place of sight. Often the stricken man does not believe it, and in his despair interprets it as a mockery. Like a drowning person he strikes blindly at anyone that tries to save him. Nevertheless, the sufferer must be urged onward in spite of himself, and when he once realizes that he can put himself again in connection with the world, and fulfill tasks worthy of a man, a being he did not dream of before unfolds itself within him. If he is wise, he discovers at last that happiness has very little to do with outward circumstances, and he treads his dark way with a firmer will than he ever felt in the light.

Helen Keller

Don't turn away from me, my friend. Don't lock me out of you life. I want your pain. Talk to me about it. I want it to be my pain, too.

I don't know why my friend and neighbor is sick and dying and in constant pain. From my religious perspective, I cannot tell him that God has His reasons for sending him this terrible fate, or that God must specially love him or admire his bravery to test him in this way. I can only tell him that the God I believe in did not send the disease and does not have a miraculous cure that He is withholding. But in a world in which we all possess immortal spirits in fragile and vulnerable bodies, the God I believe in gives strength and courage to those who, unfairly and through no fault of their own, suffer pain and the fear of death. I can help him remember that he is more than a crippled body. He is more than a man with a debilitating illness. He is a man with a loving wife and children, with many friends, and with enough iron in his soul to remain a living person in the fullest sense of the word until the very last day.

Harold S. Kushner

Prayer for the Reader

Be my Healer, Jesus. Mend me in mind and spirit as well as body, for I have great need of Your care. Give me patience, revive my hope when it flickers feebly, and build in me such a trust in Your will for me that I will meet each day of my life with the knowledge that I will find in it a blessing.

WHEN SOMEONE CAN'T STOP DRINKING

"Look upon mine affliction and my pain; and forgive all my sins. . . .
O keep my soul, and deliver me."

(Psalm 25:18, 20, KJV)

You've tried—everything. You've been sympathetic, understanding, patient, forgiving, supportive. Then angry, harsh, silent, accusing. And now you blame yourself. Maybe it *is* your fault. Maybe you're driving your alcoholic to drink, as he or she claims you are. But you're exhausted from believing him when he promises to stop, and then doesn't. Your capacity to hope has been crushed too many times. And that funny little smile on his face when you tell him for the umpteenth time how much he has hurt you. It's almost as if he *wants* you to scream at him. To cry and bite your lip. To despise yourself for saying such things to him.

Your suspicions may be true. Your alcoholic—he or she—may *want* you to say out loud all the terrible things he or she says to himself deep down inside. The reason is that the alcoholic has a serious problem besides the need to drink: he hates himself, and he believes everyone else does, or ought to. He wants you to confirm his poor opinion of himself, and he may not be able to hear anything else you say.

But you have a problem, too. The more patient you are, the more closely you watch over your alcoholic, you cannot stop him or her from drinking. The harder you try, the worse the problem—yours and your alcoholic's—will get. What started out as a loving embrace is now your stranglehold on each other.

The alcoholic needs help. But so does the person who loves one. And they cannot help each other because their human emotions, their self-doubts, their confusion, get in the way. If ever there were a situation where God has to get into the act, it is this tragic relationship.

> Where do you get the strength to go on, when you have used up all of your own strength? Where do you turn for patience when you have run out of patience, when you have been more

patient for more years than anyone should be asked to be, and the end is nowhere in sight? I believe that God gives us strength and patience and hope, renewing our spiritual resources when they run dry. How else do sick people manage to find more strength and more good humor over the course of prolonged illness than any one person could possibly have, unless God was constantly replenishing their souls? How else do widows find the courage to pick up the pieces of their lives and go out to face the world alone, when on the day of their husband's funeral, they did not have the courage? How else do the parents of a retarded or brain-damaged youngster wake up every morning and turn again to their responsibilities, unless they are able to lean on God when they grow weak?

We don't have to beg or bribe God to give us strength or hope or patience. We need only turn to Him, admit that we can't do this on our own, and understand that bravely bearing up under long-term illness is one of the most human, and one of the most godly, things we can ever do. One of the things that constantly reassures me that God is real, and not just an idea that religious leaders made up, is the fact that people who pray for strength, hope, and courage so often find resources of strength, hope, and courage that they did not have before they prayed.

Harold S. Kushner

Very simply put, decision means making a resolution to change. We actually start moving in the direction we have taken. . . . Awareness has led us to this position, but we know that we will need help of some kind to persevere in our decision.

. . . Do prayers work? Can prayer change people?

Yes, if we concentrate more on ourselves than others.

Perhaps one reason why some of our prayers are unanswered is because we forget the other side of prayer: our side. The old proverbs point this out: "Pray, but row to shore." "Pray for potatoes, but pick up a hoe."

Prayer works if it gives us the grace to get up off our knees and do something constructive about a problem. It can lead us to reach out for marriage counseling even if our partner refuses to go. It can lead to Al-Anon, the Alcoholic Anonymous group for relatives and friends of alcoholics.

. . . Prayer works if it leads us to deeper compassion, forgiveness, and understanding of the difficult person.

Prayer works if it teaches us to keep searching to do the Father's will.

Prayer works if it gets us to start with ourselves—to search into our attitudes, our own sinfulness.

Prayer works if it causes us to ask ourselves, "How responsible are we for this problem?"

. . . Prayer works if it makes us realize that dealing with difficult people is a problem with no easy solutions, and that no self-help books alone—not even the Bible—will solve the problem. We personally must use the grace of God obtained through prayer to solve our problems with difficult people.

We need to make a statement at least to ourselves on how we will try to improve our relationships with the people around us, especially the difficult ones. We need to know ourselves better, becoming aware of our mindsets. Then we can make a *decision* to go forward with God at our side.

Andrew Costello

What you and your alcoholic need now is separation—not necessarily physical or legal separation, although that may be a decision you will want to make eventually. But your emotional ties to each other—your guilt and anger, and the alcoholic's need for your guilt and anger—must be severed. If you think of these ties as your love for each other, you are wrong, and what you both need is to experience what real love is. It does not destroy; it builds.

If you are going to do all you can to help your alcoholic recover—and that means preventing him from dying or going irretrievably insane—then you must learn to stop "helping" him. You must learn to stop rescuing the alcoholic. Learn how to stop believing, "But he's suffering so much! I *must* help him!" Because if you continue to "help" your alcoholic, you will be helping to keep him sick.

...It is very important for you to understand that the alcoholic is more dependent on you than you are on him, *although both of you live under the illusion that it's the other way around.* When you realize this truth you'll be able to take measures to get help for you and your kids. And you don't have to let go of your fears before you take action. Take action—and then the fears will drop! It's an act of faith. You have to get the courage to take that first step, in blind faith that it will all work out.

If he goes on being untreated, he will get sicker, more cruel, more mean, less kind, less responsible—those characteristics are part and parcel of this progressive disease called alcoholism. Alcoholism doesn't get better by just praying, by standing still and hoping it will go away. You have to take action. You must *do* something. And if you do something to get help, that action will affect the alcoholic in a positive way. No family member can remain unaffected by another family member getting help and getting better.

Toby Rice Drews

I am no longer sorry that I sent that letter to you, though I was very sorry for a time, realizing how painful it would be to you. But it hurt you only for a little while. Now I am glad I sent it, not because it hurt you, but because the pain turned you to God. It was a good kind of sorrow you felt, the kind of sorrow God wants his people to have...to help us turn away from sin and seek eternal life.

(II Corinthians 7:8–10, Living Bible)

By cutting your emotional dependency on each other, you will create a space between you where Christ can enter. And, believe me, His is the only kind of love that can heal either one of you. Yes, *you* need healing, too, and you cannot really help your alcoholic until you are whole. It isn't easy.

> ...My love may be "tough" love, not at all sweet and coddling. You may ask me for another drink when you are already inebriated, or you may ask me to join you in some deception. Of course, if I truly love you, I must say an emphatic "No!" to these requests. If you are on a self-destructive course, like alcoholism, you will meet in me a firm and confronting love. But, when needed, my love will also be "tender." If you have tried and failed, and you just need a hand in yours in the darkness of disappointment, you can count on mine.
>
> *John Powell*

And if you are the alcoholic, it's going to take you a long time to believe that you are loved. Because believing it means the end of your self-abusing ways, and right now that is the only way of life you know. You're going to need a great deal of courage to let go of what you do know and dare to step out into a world that is unfamiliar. Love will make demands on you. Self-respect can hurt.

> How many of us really want life, life more abundant, life which does not promise any fringe benefits or early retirement plans? Life which does not promise the absence of pain, or love which is not vulnerable and open to hurt? The number of people who attempt to withdraw from life through the abuse of alcohol, tranquilizers, barbiturates, is statistically shocking.
>
> *Madeleine L'Engle*

The fear of not succeeding is, for many people, the biggest obstacle in their way. It holds them back from trying anything at all. And for lack of trying they never give themselves a chance of succeeding—the very thing that would cure them of their doubts. It is not, after all, such a terrible thing not to succeed straightaway in some new undertaking. What is serious is to give up, to become stuck in a life that just gets emptier.

Paul Tournier

There was a man who was severely handicapped. He could think of a lot of things he wanted to do, but his hand was withered. He could not translate his thoughts into deeds. The hand represents action and his hand was withered. . . .

I have talked with many people who have a liquor problem. But I have never talked with any who weren't quick to say it was hurting their lives and they were going to give it up. But so often their hands are withered. They can't quite carry out their good thoughts. They lack the power to translate their desires into actions. . . .

Look into your own mind and see how many good things you have there which you have thought about doing. But as yet you haven't had the right opportunity, or you lack the ability, or you don't have enough training, and haven't had time, or you don't feel like it—all those excuses are just other names for your handicap of a withered hand. You think well but you don't act.

To the man with the withered hand Jesus said, "Stand forth." That is, you have drifted long enough. Now let's face up to the situation. There comes a time when we must take command of our thoughts.

Charles L. Allen

You're like the children of Israel emerging from the wilderness and looking off into the distance at the land of milk and honey. There it is, and suddenly it isn't wonderful anymore, but terrifyingly unknown. You're shaking. The dark shadows of the wilderness at your back now seem comforting. What you once thought was a prison now seems like shelter.

146

Will you go forth? If you do, you will not go alone. But the decision is up to you.

What would God want with me?

One thing: God wants to love us freely. When He is kept at arms' length, His love is there, but we refuse it. I doubt that anyone has ever understood what God's love causes Him to do. I doubt that anyone will ever understand what God's love causes Him to be. But anyone can experience that love, because everyone is welcome to His heart—*without one plea.*

The alcoholic on Skid Row is as welcome as the cultivated churchwoman. And the cultivated churchwoman is as welcome as the alcoholic on Skid Row. The self-righteous religionist is as welcome to enter into the presence of God of the universe as the prostitute. The prostitute is as welcome to enter into the presence of God as the self-righteous religionist. It is, of course, easier for the alcoholic on Skid Row and the prostitute to come—to bring themselves. Their adoration may come alive more quickly because they don't feel they have brought God much. But all are welcome—*just as they are.*

Eugenia Price

Prayer for the Reader

I feel so empty, Lord, and in need of so many strengths. But I also know I cannot even make good use of all You would give me. There is something I need more than any other gift: my faith in myself. I need to believe that You can love me, so that I can love myself, and this is very hard for me to do. Help me to see myself as You see me. That will be my beginning.

LOSING A JOB

"For yet a very little while, and the indignation shall cease."

(Isaiah 10:25, KJV)

He was trying to be kind. "You have a lot of abilities," he said. "They just aren't what we need in this job."

I was fired. "It happens to everybody at one time or another," he said, but that didn't help. It had never happened to me and I thought it never would. I had tried so hard to be a good secretary because I needed a job badly. But in all honesty, my typing was terrible—fast, but full of errors. I tried to make up for my lack of shorthand by writing fast—and then I couldn't read what I wrote. In time I might have done better, but I didn't have time.

So I dove into the classified ads. I read every one of them until I knew them by heart. Then one day I found something I thought I could do. A publishing house needed a person who wanted to learn how to edit manuscripts. Beginner okay. At a very low salary, of course. But it was better than nothing.

Yes, I got the job, and I have been in publishing ever since. Obviously it was the right place for me to be. But I wouldn't have known it if I hadn't been fired. And if the man who fired me hadn't been kind as well as honest. I *did* have abilities—we all do—but I wasn't using them in the best possible way. I was trying to fake a talent I didn't have.

Getting fired is a cruel experience and I don't wish it on anyone. Nevertheless, if it happens, it can make a difference if we remember that we are losing a job, not ourselves. No matter what the reason for the job termination, God still believes in us and so should we.

> I think one thing we must learn after becoming serious as Christians is to fail for the Lord's sake. Humanly we desire success. It is tempting to blame this longing on modern values, but I suspect this problem has plagued human beings from the beginning. As Christians we must learn that success consists in choosing the Lord's way instead of our own. . . .we must let go,

unmake ourselves. We must learn that this unmaking is not a once-for-all choice but a learning that takes place only through practice and repetition.

Emilie Griffin

"It was terrible going on interviews after I lost my job," I once heard a man confide to a friend. "I felt as if I wasn't worth two cents." It's very hard not to feel that way when you think no one wants you. That's why it is important to spend a lot of time in God's company when you begin to feel you have been rejected as an unfit human being. Let Him be your first interview.

The loss of a job can actually push you in a direction that is better for you. Or it may cause you to look back over your performance and find ways to improve it. Or it may have nothing to do with you if your employer sold the business, moved it, or simply gave it up. Your job ended. *You* didn't.

God gave us the capacity to dream, to hope and to aspire. But sometimes we do not realize our dreams; our hopes are dashed to the ground; our fondest ambitions are thwarted. Then we know the pain of disappointment and frustration. On the other hand, we also have the possibility of knowing the thrill of achievement. In order to have the possibility of one we must be willing to accept the possibility of the other.

Charles L. Allen

Prayer for the Reader

You are the only One Who can give me sympathy without making me feel sorry for myself, Lord. I need Your tenderness now, but I know You will also give me a shove to get going again. This time, though, I want to rely more on Your sense of direction. I didn't do so well on my own.

SHARING THE BURDEN:
Meeting the Needs of Others

God brings us out into the world and gives us
understanding, compassion, trust. . . .

COMMITTING TO ANOTHER

"I remember you,
The kindness of your youth,
The love of your betrothal,
When you went after Me in the wilderness."

(Jeremiah 2:2, NKJV)

They were my ideal couple. Now in their seventies, they had been married for decades. Each one had remained a complete person, fiercely so, and their support of each other came as much out of respect as loyalty. If anyone had asked me, I couldn't have told you which I admired more, Roger or Louise.

But age and illness were taking their toll. First, it was Roger; a serious heart condition that required careful living, a hard task for a man of such mental energy. Then Louise; her spine would never be right again, and she bristled at the prospect of wearing a brace.

I was uncomfortable when I was with them. Gone were their usual lively stands, sometimes on opposite sides of an issue. Instead they were cranky with each other, complaining, obsessed with minor inconveniences. Roger was tired of keeping the house neat while Louise was confined to bed.

150

Louise was all for moving into a retirement community, but Roger wouldn't hear of it. Bicker, bicker, bicker.

And then I saw it—the concern in Louise's eyes when Roger stopped to get his breath. Roger's shaky hand coming down gently over Louise's after she tried once more to get out of bed and couldn't. It was still there: the love. The bliss, the headlong plunge of emotion, the heartbeat flushing the temples, were long since gone. But the commitment was still there.

My love for my wife is not blown back and forth by the winds of change, by circumstances and environmental influences. Even though my fickle emotions jump from one extreme to another, my commitment remains solidly anchored. I have chosen to love my wife, and that choice is sustained by an uncompromising will.

The essential investment of commitment is sorely missing in so many modern marriages. I love you, they seem to say, as long as I feel attracted to you—or as long as someone else doesn't look better—or as long as it is to my advantage to continue the relationship. Sooner or later, this unanchored love will certainly vaporize.

"For better or worse, for richer, for poorer, in sickness and in health, to love, and to cherish, till death us do part. . ."

That familiar pledge from the past still offers the most solid foundation upon which to build a marriage, for therein lies the real meaning of genuine romantic love.

James Dobson

Commitment. What is this word, *commitment*? I love you with all my heart and mind and soul. Isn't that enough?

No.

Commitment speaks another language. I will not always find it easy to love you, it says. There will be times when I will lose interest in you, when you will annoy me and try my patience. I will even begin to hate you, although I hope those times will not last long enough to destroy our love. We will argue sometimes, you and I, and our differences will not always be healed. We will often be as distant as we are close. I will have to deal with these intrusions on our serentiy, our joy in each other, our passion, comfort and devotion—and so will you. At those times love will not always feel like a throbbing heart; it may be very quiet, very steady, but not exactly exciting. But it will be there. That is when love will be at its strongest.

...It is our sense of commitment after the wedding which makes possible the transition from falling in love to genuine love. And it is our commitment after conception which transforms us from biological into psychological parents. Commitment is inherent in any genuinely loving relationship. Anyone who is truly concerned for the spiritual growth of another knows, consciously or instinctively, that he or she can significantly foster that growth only through a relationship of constancy. Children cannot grow to psychological maturity in an atmosphere of unpredictability, haunted by the specter of abandonment. Couples cannot resolve in any healthy way the universal issues of marriage or dependency and independency, dominance and submission, freedom and fidelity, for example —without the security of knowing that the act of struggling over these issues will not itself destroy the relationship.

M. Scott Peck

The Old Testament uses the word *covenant* to describe the special promises and commitments that bind husband and wife together...By *covenant* we mean more than agreements about who walks the dog and how towels get folded. The promises implicit in convenant include cherishing one another, respecting one another fully, putting the other's welfare ahead of one's own, forgiveness, and the choice to love that transcends the day-to-day inconveniences, petty annoyances, and disappointments of living under the same roof year after year.

We rarely take the time—and the risk—of exploring and affirming this deeper level of relationship. We listen to the chatter of life around us, but how often do we *really listen* to the heart and soul of our partner? How often do you turn your ears on and focus exclusively on trying to know and understand your partner fully?

Donald A. Tubesing and Nancy Loving Tubesing

Commitment is Christ in Gethsemane, dreading the pain of love but willing to accept it. It is beauty losing its hair and taking on wrinkles, remembering the bliss, yes, but knowing something more wonderful has grown in its place. It is love daring to live honestly, to meet change, to bear burdens, to gain insights, to trust its own strength. It is an old man's trembling hand on the pain-gnarled hand of his wife; it is her eyes watching his spasm-hunched shoulders.

The falling part is over. Commitment is love with its feet on the ground.

Prayer for the Reader

I want my existence to mean something in the life of another, Lord. I want to care as well as be cared about. That kind of love isn't easy, is it, Lord? Life has so many ways of testing love—dreams that don't come true, broken promises, worry, illness, other loyalties, other attractions, responsibilities. Teach me the kind of love that grows stronger with use.

BEING A WIFE

"May the Lord God . . . under whose wings you have come to take refuge, bless you. . . ."

(Ruth 2:12, Living Bible)

My mother was a very good wife, but she never realized it. She thought she was a failure, not only because her first marriage ended in divorce, but because she didn't fit into the traditional role of a wife in her day.

She was a little ahead of her time. She worked, for one thing, and none of my friends' mothers worked. None of my stepfather's friends' wives worked either.

She hired a housekeeper to clean our house because she wanted it to be spotless and she didn't have time to dust and vacuum. None of my friends' mothers did that. Or my stepfather's friends' wives.

But my mother did all the cooking. As a family we were up earlier than most because my mother not only had to get me off to school and my stepfather off to work, but she had to get to work, too. Still, she made us all a big breakfast every morning because she wanted us to be strong and healthy and have plenty of energy to get us through the day. We took time to talk before we went our separate ways. She even made my lunch for school five days a week, and my brown bag had some of the best goodies you ever saw. None of your freezer sandwiches for me—mine had fresh lettuce and bread spread with butter or mayonnaise and filled with some of last night's chicken or roast beef. Best of all was when my mother gave me a thermos of her homemade vegetable soup, thick with carefully cut-up carrots and onions and turnips and potatoes and stringbeans and tomatoes, and aromatic with herbs and long-simmered broth.

> . . .The loving individual has to care about himself. This is number one. I don't mean an ego trip. I'm talking about somebody who really cares about himself, who says, "Everything is filtered through me, and so the greater I am, the more I have to give. The greater knowledge I have, the more I'm going to

have to give. The greater understanding I have, the greater is my ability to teach others and to make myself the most fantastic, the most beautiful, the most wondrous, the most tender human being in the world."

Leo Buscaglia

My mother didn't take me to school. I walked there, usually teaming up with friends along the way. In those days it wasn't considered exacting for a child to walk a mile or so to school, and even in bad weather I enjoyed it. Rain was a dare, snow was all kinds of games, cool sunny days meant skipping and, then, after school, jumping rope, and hot sun meant vacation was on the way. Who could complain? Certainly not I.

But my mother always felt guilty about preferring a job outside our home. In the early days of their marriage, when my stepfather was climbing up the corporate ladder, my mother could rationalize that we needed the extra money. Then, when my stepfather was doing well, my mother said she couldn't quit her job because her boss needed her. In fact, she did quit a few times and her boss begged her to return, which she was only too happy to do because being home with a child in school all day was not enough of a challenge to her.

Jesus stands for reverence for the personality of the woman. In one place it is said of Jesus, "He laid his hands upon her: and immediately she was made straight." When the hands of a good deal of modern teaching are laid on woman, immediately she is made crooked. Jesus insisted that she must not be a means to man's ends, but that she is an end in herself, and must be treated as such.

E. Stanley Jones

That first winter, with snow piled four feet high outside the front door, was a long one. My husband was busy looking after the needs of a fast-growing community. Like other young mothers, I found myself isolated for long periods of the day without any adult contact. In the city, I had managed to carry a part-time job which gave me an outside interest. Where we now lived, there was no opportunity to work in my particular field, and even if there had been, it was impossible to find a daytime babysitter.

In my loneliness I turned to prayer and discovered that God really is a friend. And in that growing relationship, I made another discovery. Until then my dealings with God had always been on the level of a child talking to her Father. Now I found that we also communicated on the level of one parent talking to another. There were times when I might be concerned with some particular fault in my children, and then I'd realize that God had the same fault to deal with in me. It gave me an entirely new outlook on life.

Marcia Hollis

My stepfather put up with a lot of not-so-subtle remarks from his men friends about letting his wife work. He never got his dander up about it. Maybe he was a little ahead of his time, too, but he always used to walk over to my mother at times like that and give her a little kiss on top of her head, which sometimes surprised her, especially if she was in the middle of talking to someone.

"What's that for?" she would say to him.

"Nothing," he would answer and move off.

And that's what the kiss was for: indeed, nothing. Not for anything special or out of the ordinary. My stepfather was not a man of many words, but his actions made it quite clear that he thought my mother was a very good wife. I only wish she had realized that in time.

Not too long ago in a couples group I heard one of the members state that the "purpose and function" of his wife was to keep their house neat and him well fed. I was aghast at what seemed to me his painfully blatant male chauvinism. I thought I might demonstrate this to him by asking the other members of the group to state how they perceived the purpose and function of their spouses. To my horror the six others, male and female alike, gave very similar answers. All of them defined the purpose and function of their husbands or wives in reference to themselves; all of them failed to perceive that their mates might have an existence basically separate from their own or any kind of destiny apart from their marriage. "Good grief," I exclaimed, "it's no wonder that you are all having difficulties in your marriages, and you'll continue to have difficulties until you come to recognize that each of you has your own separate destiny to fulfill." The group felt not only chastised but profoundly confused by my pronouncement. Somewhat belligerently they asked me to define the purpose and function of my wife. "The purpose and function of Lily," I responded, "is to grow to be the most of which she is capable."

M. Scott Peck

Finally, it got to her, this business of being a working wife. She spoke of it often to me, wondering if it was fair to me for her to be away from home every day, and to give people the impression that my stepfather couldn't provide for his family without her help. I never knew what to say because, frankly, I had enough trouble fencing with the not-so-subtle remarks from the mothers of my friends about my mother who worked. As far as I was concerned, neither my stepfather nor I had suffered from her not being at home all day while we were away. And during the few times she had "retired" I found my mother quite hard to take because she was so depressed.

Anyway, a strange thing happened when I finished college. My mother decided to stay home. This time she really quit and wouldn't go back to work. And that was the end of her.

She lost all confidence in herself. One day when I asked her to type a resumé for me, she tried and failed, miserably—and this was a woman who was one of the best typists in history. "My fingers are stiff," she said, but that wasn't it. She was scared.

She began to drink. Heavily. She tried to hide it, but we all knew. We consulted doctors, treatment centers, A.A., and none of them worked. My stepfather's career was very demanding by then, and I left home to get married. My mother was alone—doing her best to be a good wife, and nobody around to appreciate it.

She's still alone. There is nothing my stepfather or I can do or say to get through to her in her terrible isolation. And all I can do is pray that, somehow, God can. She needs to know that, even though she found different ways to do it, she was a very good wife. And mother.

I wish my mother had been closer to God during those years. I wish she had learned something I learned, a long time later, after I almost made the same mistakes she did.

What I'm getting at is that there is no one shape or form or standard of behavior that determines what a wife is. What matters is that a woman has the ability to understand the needs of her family. Who does the dishes, who cooks the meals, or even who writes the checks to pay the bills, isn't important. What counts is the care and love that will see to it that these things, and more, are done. And what really counts is the reverence of a woman for the individuals in her care, and the realization that she has them in her charge for only a small part of their lives. In truth, they belong to God, and a wife is God's way of caring for them in human terms.

> . . . Most of life, because of the changepoints, represents an ongoing adjustment period.
>
> Consider this for a moment. About the time I got over the hideous junior-high phase of life and was finally adjusting to the roller-coaster emotions of a teenager, I turned twenty and got married. Then, before I discovered any ancient or new clues about marriage, I was up to my earlobes in babies, formulas and dirty diapers. Every time I turned around, I was dealing with yet another changepoint.
>
> . . . Then I knew that the question was not what I'll do with another changepoint, but what *He* will do.

...When do I need Him most? Ah, the gentle conviction became stronger, and I began to understand that there is not one certain time of life, not one particular phase of growth during which we need God more than any other. All of life—each stage and each moment—is in fact a never-ending time of needing the Lord.

Joyce Landorf

Prayer for the Reader

Enable me, Lord, to feel comfortable with myself. Don't let me be intimidated by customs and trends that are here one day and gone the next. Let me learn loving care from You rather than from the world.

BEING A HUSBAND

"I will instruct you and teach you in the way you should go; I will guide you with My eye."

(Psalm 32:8, NKJV)

If Jesus had wanted only to carry out His earthly mission on our behalf, He never would have bothered to gather disciples around Him. They would have got in His way, taken up His time and claimed His involvement in their lives. How much more efficient it would have been for Him to do what He came to do and get it over with. But no, He formed relationships, lasting ones. He became an intimate part of the lives of those He loved. Still, He completed what He came to do, and perhaps the gift of life His death achieved for us has an even greater significance because He showed us, while He was with us, how rich that life could be.

There never was a busier man than Jesus Christ, Son of God, come into this world to save mankind from sin and death. Harried by Roman conquerors, stung and reviled by the captive Israelites, urged by His followers to proclaim Himself a king, He could yet hear the smothered cry of a sorrowing heart. With so few years in which to say all He hungered to make known to us, with no more hours in the day than we have now, He could yet stop to rest a while along the way, or in the home of friends. As urgent as His mission was, He could yet laugh and make small talk, or sit quietly, listening for that unspoken "I need you" in the conversation around Him. It's amazing what small concerns people brought to Him in the midst of monumental events. And He could give them His attention.

Study our Lord's life. You will see He knew something about the everyday struggle to make ends meet. He knew the meaning of the widow's two mites, what a disaster the loss of a coin might be, wearing clothes which were patched. He knew about shopping in the grocery store to try to stretch a budget to feed the family. He talks about the housewife who must buy two birds which sold for a penny.

Charles L. Allen

160

Jesus was a Person who taught by doing, by being. He didn't lecture. He described only what He was, only what God gave Him the grace to be. He was so incredibly, miraculously ordinary. There was no harshness in the Man, no arrogance or trappings of power. Only the strength that comes from the willingness and courage to feel, to understand, to be close to—without apology.

So it is—or can be—with a husband.

One of the good things to come out of the recent turmoil over the roles of a man and a woman is the awareness that a husband can't do everything. Nor should he even try. Yet most men do try; it's the way they were brought up. They try to imitate God, or at least what they assume God does. They try to create a world, people it, and then see to it that everything runs smoothly. When it becomes apparent that they need help, they delegate tasks to members of their family. Now, *certainly*, everything will run smoothly.

But then, when their world develops cracks and even huge holes in its foundation, their wives and children point fingers at them and tell them they didn't do enough, or they didn't do the right things, and it's all their fault.

We seem to have accepted money as the cure-all for every disease, need, or problem imaginable. A man who has not said one real thing to his wife in years shrugs his shoulders and says, "I don't know what she wants—she's got everything. She can go out and buy anything. She's got the house, clothes, and tons of *things*. What else does she need?" He has made the money, bought the myth, and paid for it. All he has to show for himself is a large brick wall made up of material possessions which stand solidly between him and his wife. He thought his money would buy a bridge; instead it has built a wall, but his intention and efforts were sincere.

Joyce Landorf

Our trouble is that we are less certain of God's will than Jesus Christ was. And the danger of being mistaken is always greatest at the moment when we flatter ourselves that we know his will. At that point we are already falling into the error of magic, claiming to penetrate the secrets of God. But without ever being sure that we know in advance what God requires of us, we may never stop humbly seeking his will.

Paul Tournier

It's very difficult to be a husband. Especially when most men are following the wrong role model.

In the first place, God is not a stern administrator, a bringer home of bread, and a charger-up of hills too high for any mortal to climb. He is a loving, communicating Father Who knows what is going on in the lives of all His children. And because He does understand how difficult it is to be a husband—to be both friend and lover to a wife, shelterer and teacher to children—God has provided the perfect role model: Jesus Christ. That's right, the Example most often overlooked by men who are desperately seeking answers to the question: What is a husband?—especially these days? Never mind which day it is, or how the world turns; the meaning of a husband has always been the same: Jesus.

But—Jesus didn't marry. He didn't have a wife and children. No. He had a family. He drew men, women and children to Him and they became His earthly family. We are members of it, all of us who have given our lives to Him. And when He left His family, He left us able to carry on His work, move closer to His goals, and look after His world. Our relationships with each other are part of that world, and He is still our Example. Can any husband hope to achieve more?

> Think of it! Because of God's love the world was created. Each of us was made! The thousands of hairs on our heads, the color of our eyes, everything concrete about us and the world in which we live was made because of the love of God. . .Christians, of all people, must value the earth precisely because the earth, and everything else in the cosmic order as well, originates in God's decision to love. Specifically, because of that love, the world came into being and presently exists.
>
> *Earl F. Palmer*

Jesus never tried to compete with God. He accepted Himself as God's Son, as the physical embodiment of God's spiritual love for all men and women. More than anything, He cared deeply about God's creation. He taught us how to appreciate it, how to maintain and improve it. The very word *husband* means "to make grow."

And that is what Jesus, in His earthly journey, did: He made us grow. Not with a wave of a magic wand, as fairy tales would have it. Not by edict and threat of reprimand—in fact, His only "command" was that we love one another. He made us grow by being a friend, by valuing what we are, even while He saw what we are not, by sheltering us from the destructive powers of evil, and by teaching us how to use the powers of good in our lives.

> To be honest; to be kind; to earn a little and to spend a little less; to make, upon the whole, a family happier for his presence; to renounce, when that shall be necessary, and not be embittered; to keep a few friends, but these without capitulation; above all, on the same condition, to keep friends with himself: here is a task for all that a man has of fortitude and delicacy.
>
> *Robert Louis Stevenson*

We don't think of the word *husband* as a verb these days, but it still is one. It means "to cultivate another's property"—a very revealing description of what a husband does, even now. Husbands do not own those they make grow; they do not even own themselves. They are not responsible for the outcome of their efforts; they must not and cannot make their loved ones in their own image. They can only serve God, just as their loved ones do. And when their burdens become too heavy, they can seek help from the Highest Power.

Husbands do not run this world. They work in it, side by side with those they love. Husbands are not perfect. They are superbly human.

> When you face an impossibility, leave it in the hands of the Specialist. Refuse to calculate. Refuse to doubt. Refuse to work it out by yourself. Refuse to worry or encourage others to worry. Stand against that.
>
> Instead, say, "Lord, I'm carrying around something I cannot handle. Because You are not only able but also willing and anx-

ious, take this off my hands. It's impossible to me, but it is as nothing to You." Persevering through the pressures of impossibilities calls for *that* kind of confidence.

Now, our problem is that we hold onto our problems. If your Swiss watch stops working, you don't sit down at home with a screwdriver and start working on it yourself. You take it to a specialist.

What if you do work on that watch and *then* you take it to a specialist? "Sir, my watch stopped working."

"Oh, really. Let me take a look at it. . .What in the world have you done to this lovely watch?"

The problem is that the Lord gets all the leftovers. We make all the mistakes and get things tied into nineteen granny knots, then dump it into His lap and say, "Here, Lord."

No! Right at first, say, "It's impossible: I can't handle it. Lord, before I foul it up, it's Yours." He is able to handle it.

Charles H. Swindoll

Jesus did not use words ending in "ity," which we are so fond of using. He did not talk of personality, he talked of persons. He did not ask us to love humanity, he asked us to love people.

E. Stanley Jones

Prayer for the Reader

Who am I trying to kid, Lord? There are times when I want to break down and cry, but I know I'm not supposed to do that, so I end the conversation or duck behind the newspaper or sit up late watching TV until everybody's asleep. Sometimes, then, I let You see me cry. Do You think, Lord, I may be mistaken? That maybe it's all right to cry—as You did?

STARTING A FAMILY

"Yea, thou shalt see thy children's children. . . ."

(Psalm 128:6, KJV)

Families don't just "happen" anymore. You have a choice. Or at least you can choose to have a choice. Which means you have some important matters to consider as you make your decision.

You have to figure out how you'll get along on one pay check, because now you barely get along on two. And a house—what about that? Your apartment is only big enough for the two of you. A house costs money, more than you have.

> Young couples will sometimes tell me that they are afraid to have children in these uneasy times. It may be that we are currently experiencing a measurable decline in our national birth rate because so many in our generation are apprehensive about the future. Christian love, quite to the contrary, wagers on the future.
>
> *Earl F. Palmer*

Of course, you can wait. You can prepare for the family you plan to have. Besides, you both are enjoying life the way it is. It's interesting. You're not tied down. You have time for each other.

Except that—one Saturday morning at the supermarket a little girl, not more than two years old, comes up to you and takes your hand. Maybe she thinks she belongs to you. But no, her parents are there, smiling apologetically and calling her back to them. You tell them she's no bother—you'd love to let her help push your basket.

You mean it.

Walking down the aisle between all those cans of tomatoes, peas and soup suddenly has become something special. The little hand, the tiny, sticky fingers, give you goose bumps. Something about the way she looks up at you when you talk to her makes you want to cry.

You remember another time when you walked down a different kind of aisle. In church at your wedding. You looked at each other, so much in love, but you couldn't put it into words. No, not words. But someday, out of your incredible love, would come a child. Someday.

So now you're in an aisle lined with canned food and someone else's child is making you realize that someday won't be there forever. Your love for each other is different now, too, and in some ways it's better. Yet you still can't put it into words.

And Joseph lifted him up for her to see. And they looked upon him together and marveled at him, his wholeness, infinitely small and red and perfectly formed. And when he squirmed in Joseph's arms and uttered his first cry, the thrill of all mankind ran through both of them, for this was life, human life, and they knew that a miracle had been achieved.

Marjorie Holmes

But—a child is not for the two of you alone. The child holding your hand is new life, and you are right to think about the responsibilities that come with it. Even in the best of times, new life itself is a miracle. God has a part in it—and He must have a part in any decision you make.

Raising kids is a pretty awesome task, even when the job is handled by a team of two, as intended. It can be downright terrifying when approached as a solitary endeavor. In the first place, parenthood is a guilty affair. No matter how hard one tries, it is impossible to discharge the responsibility perfectly. Children are maddeningly complicated, and *no one* has all the answers to the myriad of problems that can arise. Furthermore, both the masculine and feminine personalities are needed in modeling of roles for children. Each gender makes its own contribution to the development of little minds, and a mother knows she is

166

not equipped to play both parts. There's no doubt about it, raising children as a "single parent" (whether married or not) is the loneliest job in the world!

James Dobson

New life will mean sacrifices for the two of you. No matter how well you prepare for the family you want to start, you will have to give up more than you expect. The two of you will change in ways you can't anticipate. The best of plans will not always work out. You will need to be close to God, and so will your child. The child you want and the family you want are His, not yours. You are the custodians of His miracle. And while it is important to make your plans, you can't consider only those matters that concern you. Make room for God in the family you decide to start.

Prayer for the Reader

O, Father it's so easy to misinterpret our right to choose. We begin to believe it gives us the power to create life simply because we can say no to it. Our freedom was never meant to come between You and us, yet that can happen if we use it selfishly. We could become another Adam and Eve, trying to remodel Eden according to our own desires. Will You, instead, enter into this freedom with us and teach us how to use it in Your Kingdom?

BEING A PARENT

"Be happy. Grow in Christ. Pay attention to what I have said. Live in harmony and peace. And may the God of love and peace be with you."
(II Corinthians 13:11, Living Bible)

Did you ever hear the remark, "Being a parent is the most important job in the world, yet there isn't any course in how to do it"? A comedian said it, meaning it as a joke. But you know it isn't funny.

I celebrate children
    who laugh out loud
    who walk in the mud and dawdle in the puddles
    who put chocolate fingers anywhere
    who like to be tickled
    who scribble in church
    who whisper in loud voices
    who sing in louder voices
    who run—and laugh when they fall
    who cry at the top of their lungs
    who cover themselves with Band-Aids
    who squeeze the toothpaste all over the bathroom
    who slurp their soup
    who chew cough drops
    who ask questions
    who give us sticky, paste-covered creations
    who want their pictures taken
    who don't use their napkins
    who bury their goldfish, sleep with the dog, scream
      at their best friends
    who hug us in a hurry and rush outside without their hats.
I celebrate children who are so busy living they don't have
    time for our hangups,
And I celebrate adults who are as little children.
Ann Weems

When our children were little, I noticed that one would sometimes run into the house yelling, "Mom!" and if I happened to be on the phone my husband would automatically answer, "Yes, what is it?" Just as frequently, it would happen the other way around and I would respond to a nighttime cry of "Dad!" because I was already awake and my husband was sound asleep. And it never mattered at all to the children when this happened because what the cry really meant was, "Parent!" I think this is what happens when we pray to our heavenly Father. It is a term of relationship which God himself has taught us to use.

Marcia Hollis

Everyone tells you it's easier with the second child, but parenthood at any time is an awesome responsibility. Advice? You get too much of it, and all of it different. The best way to bring up a child yesterday is the worst way today.

Suppose you make a mistake? What will that do to your child's future development? Can you discipline your child without turning him or her against you? Are you giving your child enough room to grow? Too much? Are you demonstrating your love? Are you too demonstrative? Are you spending enough time with your child? Or too much? Who can tell you?

You can. And you must.

Like it or not, prepared or unprepared, you are the authority in your child's life. You are not your child's playmate, buddy or best friend. You are your child's guardian, God's delegate in this world. You are your child's guide to reality; the world around your child will be interpreted by you, the parent. You are your child's protector and provider of nourishment. You will receive your child's first uncertain communications; your appreciative response will build in him or her a sense of trust; your attention and encouragement will provide the soil in which his or her self-esteem will grow. Yes, you are important.

Please show me my true priorities—as a parent and as a responsible Christian. Please give me guidance, God.

Marjorie Holmes

The knowledge and love of God are life's greatest joy and privilege, but they can't be forced or hammered into anyone. So take it slow. Expose the very young child to the great, dramatic stories of the Bible; read them to him yourself. Let him see religion as a natural part of family life, a sustaining and benevolent force. In our family, when a child was facing an examination or a music recital we always said, "We'll be thinking of you," meaning really, "We'll be praying for you." Later, when the children were grown, if they knew my wife or I had to give a talk or conduct some important meeting they would often ask for the exact time and then say, "I'll be thinking of you". . . meaning the same thing.

Norman Vincent Peale

If you think that bringing up children is boring, demeaning and a waste of your talents, consider this: You will need, and use, every bit of intelligence, insight, administrative ability, athletic prowess, wit, appreciation of art, music and literature, mechanical engineering, animal husbandry, horticulture, furniture refinishing, typing, home economics, medical know-how and mechanical drafting you have learned or picked up along the way. You will be called to minister to your child's spiritual needs. You will bring God and your child together. There is no more demanding, creative or diversified job in the world than participating in the life of a new and totally unique human being.

But you won't always think so. At times you may be so consumed by your work that you won't be able to see what you are accomplishing. Or it won't seem to matter because you're so tired. Don't think God doesn't understand. He knows what exhaustion is. He knows you need rest. He hasn't put aside your needs because you have a child. And neither should you.

I will speak bluntly, though I don't intend to offend or alienate my masculine readers. If you want your wife to accept the responsibility of motherhood and all that it implies, then you must provide her with your support and involvement. You must let her talk to you when she has had a difficult day with the children, offering suggestions and alternative approaches; you must help her discipline and train and guide; you must meet her emotional and romantic needs which accumulate in your absence; you must understand her requirement to get away from her small children at least once a week; and, most important, you must reserve some of your time for your family.

James Dobson

Parenting is not a matter of the hours you put in on the job. Sometimes it isn't a matter of how well you do your job, but that you do it with care. With love. "Short shrift," my great-grandmother used to say when she was trying to take care of me with one hand and doing six other things with the other.

From time to time, young and weary mother, you are going to yell the wrong response, attack when you should be still, lose any semblance of self-control, and make a first-class mess of things. But take heart! God is in control, even though you're probably too tired to notice, and best of all, He's growing you into a special mother.

Without sounding like a forty-nine-year-old Pollyanna-type woman, believe me when I say I know how God works. I know how He shapes and molds His clay children, and if you trust Him right now—babies and all—you'll not merely live through *this changepoint*, but later you'll look back and shout, "Well, what do you know? I *did do* some things right, after all!" And it will come to you loud and clear that God was right in there all the time.

Joyce Landorf

My stepfather was not my biological parent, and at times he must have felt clumsy in the role of my father. At least it seemed so to me. But he cared very much about my well-being. That was particularly evident one Christmas many years ago when my mother was in the hospital recuperating from a long illness. I used to visit her every afternoon after school and my stepfather spent the evenings with her. I would go home, make dinner for myself and get to my homework. When my stepfather came home I always had a glass of milk with him while he ate the dinner I kept warm in the oven.

Although Christmas offered us special hope in a spiritual sense that year, none of us was thinking in terms of Christmas presents. We were just glad my mother was getting well and would soon be home with us. I had bought a gift for each of my parents, but I had no thoughts about a tree or presents under it.

I'll never know how my stepfather found the time to do it, but he managed to gather up a lot of gifts, little ones that didn't cost very much. And he wrapped them most beautifully and put them under the tree. Yes, a tree—which he brought home late on Christmas Eve and decorated from top to bottom. On Christmas morning he tried to make the elaborate breakfast my mother always made for the holidays and he burned most of it. I ate it with tears in my eyes and when I told my stepfather it was delicious, I was telling the truth. We put our gifts into shopping bags and took them to my mother in the hospital. There, like three little children, we tore off the wrappings and opened the boxes.

I have never had such presents! The fleece-lined bright red mittens I had wanted for so long. Thick-ribbed socks, perfect for ice skating. A roll of transparent tape and a holder, to put on my desk. (Very grown-up). A pen. Two handkerchiefs with my initials on them. A classy looking three-ring binder to replace my tattered one—and paper refills! Nothing extravagant. But all of them what I wanted. How did my stepfather *know*? I couldn't remember telling him. Or my mother.

Parents *do* have a way of knowing their children. It comes with the job of being a parent—*if* we allow God to share our parenting with us.

Prayer for the Reader

As much as my children depend on me, Lord, I depend on You. Give me the steadiness and strength they need when mine runs short.

GETTING ALONG WITH IN-LAWS

"...*If a household is divided against itself, it cannot last.*"

(Mark 3:25, Phillips)

Two families coming together. Two ways of life. There will be conflicts. You can be sure of that. You and your life partner are drawn to each other by your attraction and devotion, by the new sense of family the two of you are creating. The newness itself binds you to each other, supports you during times of conflict and abrasion.

It is not the same with the parents, the brothers and sisters, you both left yet never completely gave up. They have one foot in your world—invited, yes, but not quite sure where they should sit or stand, how they should speak, or whether they should speak at all. They approach your new family not by attraction but by obligation. They love one of you. They aren't sure how they feel about the other. Such things take time. Will you allow them that?

And will they allow you? They approach you with arms outstretched. But for whom? You know of their love for your life partner. But will they love you? *Must* you love them?

>   ...Stop thinking of your marriage partner's relatives as a special breed known as in-laws (a term with faintly unpleasant connotations) and think of them simply as human beings with flaws and imperfections but also lovable qualities. Just discard the in-law label in your mind. Think of them as people. Treat them like people!
>
> *Ruth Stafford Peale*

>   Labels are distancing phenomena. They push us away from each other...Does he love? Does he care? What about his kids? Has he cried? Is he lonely? Is he beautiful? Is he happy? Is he giving something to someone? These are the important things.
>
> *Leo Buscaglia*

We should talk, look, listen to each other. . .we are too often silent.

Judy Collins

You do not like this business of being forced to love. You can't. Neither can they. Understand that. As you realize your own anxieties, have mercy on theirs. You are not as far apart as you may think.

But if there is discord, what then?

Your choices are limited, aren't they? Loving your life partner, can you reject those your partner loves? Not without a severe penalty. Not without some loss of love between the two of you.

We can run away from others, but we can't run away from ourselves. If we never learn to assert our thoughts and feelings, we may appear tranquil on the outside, but we are tormented from within. Those who let off steam may make mistakes, but they are probably healthier than those who don't. . . .

Andrew Costello

This is no ordinary conflict in a relationship. You cannot stand your ground, insist on your sovereignty, disengage yourself. Nor can you pretend there is peace when there is no peace.

You can—you must—become a peacemaker.

Conflict requires two points of view; peace can be made by one. Not by one knuckling under to the demands of another, but by one who is totally assured that he or she is already loved. That person asks nothing in return for the love given.

. . .If we are to be peacemakers, then we must be at peace with ourselves. The peace Jesus leaves with us has little to do with feeling good inside, much less with assurance of a calm, unruffled life or a successful career. The peace given by a crucified Messiah would not manifest itself in trivialities. No, the peace of Jesus has to do with fidelity toward the Father, with the awareness that we are loved and accepted by God... Thus grounded in what is most real, the love of God, we are able to reach out to others in peace. Because we need not find our center in pleasure, possessions or power, we have no conflict with others over the world and the things of the world. Not needing to possess or use others as assurances of our own worth, we are able to freely see them for what they are—God's children—and to place ourselves at their service.

Luke Timothy Johnson

The New Testament word for *peace*...does not mean simply the absence of conflict. It is the peace Jesus spoke of when He said, "Peace be with you" and "Go in peace." It describes a new relationship, something qualitatively different, between God and His people, and between persons. And once we have this "different" peace, it never leaves us, no matter what happens in our lives or in the world around us. God's very own peace is an occupancy of the heart, a feeling that Someone is deep inside us all the time—a spiritual reaching out for God's hand and finding it there. That is peace.

...When Jesus lives within us, His love brings the warring elements of our selves together into the whole persons we were meant to be. He frees us to be the "you" of you and the "me" of me. We can shake hands with ourselves, and we have peace.

There's also something about inner peace that makes us want to spread it around. We want to bring it into our relationships with other people and eliminate the barriers between us. But that isn't always easy, and sometimes the process isn't what we usually think of as "peaceful." It may mean uncomfortable, even painful exchanges between us.

Colleen Townsend Evans

Jesus gave us a great example of attitude and action. His attitude was one of tenderness, kindness, and forgiveness. His action was comparable, yet also very tough at times. He drove the

175

moneychangers out of the temple with whips. He lambasted the religious leaders for their hypocrisy. Jesus was tough and tender.

Along with our forgiving spirit, there is a place for a tough "No. What you are doing is wrong. I can't let you continue to do that."

Ray Burwick

Where there is love, there can be no threat to one's well-being. When there is love, there is no need to exchange grudge for grudge. Love can negotiate an area of peace where even the most antagonistic persons can dwell without hostility.

Prayer for the Reader

Make me great of heart, Lord; but first fill my heart with Your love so that I can withstand all barbs, all slights; deflect all blows to my ego. Let me not even see critical glances or hear a certain edge in a voice. O, Lord, my in-laws are coming to visit—and I really want to learn how to enjoy them!

SETTLING DIFFERENCES

"Watch out that no bitterness takes root among you, for as it springs up it causes deep trouble."

(Hebrews 12:15, Living Bible)

I will not always feel the same way about you. I will not always praise everything you do or say or think. I will not always overlook the disappointment I find in you. And I fully expect that you will not always think I am perfect. We will have our differences, won't we?

When that happens, I hope I will not feel as if you have betrayed me. I hope I will realize that you are not criticizing me or the way I live, but rather that some of your needs are different from mine. Perhaps your expectations will change as you grow and cope with life. That will happen to me, too, and you will have to adapt to my differences.

What will we do then? Will we meet each other halfway, each of us giving up a part of ourselves? Or will we find a way to honor what is unique in each of us? Will we agree to occasional moments of annoyance and discomfort with what we oppose in each other? Will we be open about our anger? Will I sometimes be more patient than you are? And sometimes will it work the other way around?

Through the years, Martha and Bob have had periods when they wished they'd never met, never married, and especially never had children. At times Bob has been angry about his disintegrating income after paying tuition bills, and sometimes has thought wistfully of a lovely South Sea island where he could take up beachcombing. Martha has occasionally gone off by herself for a good cry, and sometimes for a weekend or a day she has completely turned her back on her family and on their various needs and demands.

They've also learned that their relationship has changed from wildly exciting to warmly glowing—with an occasional exciting flash. And they can laugh together over the change in their responses to one another. Through it all, they have maintained their sense of humor, and they have both been ready to change in order to adjust to each other's needs.

Alan Loy McGinnis

Will we, at all times, allow the other to be? And if we can't, will one of us have the courage to refuse to be made over into the image of the other?

. . . My family lives with a father and husband who is still too rigid. When Ann calls for dinner and I leave my very significant activity, I expect the food to be on the table ready to serve. Quite often it's still in the process. "Now who does she think she is—keeping his eminence waiting?" And when I'm in my rigid mood, I sure let her know of the terrible inconvenience she has caused me! How would you like to live with someone like that?

Ann has a choice of response to my rigidity—anger, or love and acceptance. Her prayer at that moment can be "God, change that turkey so he'll be more pleasant to live with," or, "Lord, you are the grace I need now to forgive Ray, to love him, and accept him as he is. Work through me the gentleness I need now to confront him lovingly with the rigidity which makes him unhappy."

Ann and I have covenanted that we will not ask God to change the other until He has finished using that particular irritation to "perfect" us. Ann would pray, "Lord, don't change Ray's rigidness until You are finished using it to reshape and build me."

Ray Burwick

Our love for each other will be different, too. Quieter, perhaps, although it may occasionally speak in a harsh voice. But it will be a better kind of love, more honest, more generous, and much more forgiving. In fact, as we make room for our differences, we may begin to love each other very much as Jesus loves.

Prayer for the Reader

I know it takes courage to change, Jesus, but I need courage to accept changes in those I love. I am afraid of these differences. Not because I find anything wrong with them, but because they are unfamiliar to me. I am accustomed to a long and cherished relationship. I know all its touchy areas and how to avoid them. Now I must enter new territory, and I am nervous about it. There is, in this person I love, a bit of a stranger. And I would like to make a new friend.

WHEN SOMEONE STEALS

"If anyone is stealing he must stop it and begin using those hands of his for honest work so he can give to others in need."

(Ephesians 4:28, Living Bible)

"It's a stage you go through. Everybody does."

"They've got plenty more. They won't even miss it."

"So—I took it. So what?"

"I just wanted to see if I could do it."

I won't tell you her real name, although she wouldn't object if I did. She's not trying to hide anything. Not anymore.

But I'll call her Diana. The name suits her—lovely, dignified, well-mannered, certainly not the kind you'd ever pick as a shoplifter.

That's what she was, all right. She didn't have to steal; she had a good job and came from a comfortable home. But she didn't call it stealing, either.

"I just *took* things. I used to see other people doing it, especially in the supermarkets. I saw the same man almost every week—he'd come into the store wearing a big, loose raincoat. And he'd walk past the cigarettes and stick a whole carton under his coat.

"My friends used to take little cans of fancy goods—caviar, lobster—just for the fun of it. They thought I was stuffy because I didn't do it. Finally, I did. And I got away with it. So I did it again. One day I walked out of a store with twenty dollars' worth of merchandise I didn't pay for. That was the day I got caught."

Diana was stopped in the parking lot. The store manager and a security guard asked her to open her great big purse, and when she did, there it was: stolen goods.

"I thought I was going to die," Diana said. "I felt so—tainted. I didn't like myself. I tried to tell the manager that I wasn't really a thief, but he pointed to the food I had taken and asked me what else I would call it. He had films of me taking things off the shelves at other times. They had been watching me for a long time. I could glance at myself in the mirror and convince myself that I didn't look like a thief. But I couldn't fool those hidden cameras."

The manager was a compassionate man. He said he would not press charges if Diana agreed to pay for what she had stolen—not only on that day, but as far back as she could remember. Yes, of course, she would. But, the manager stipulated, not all at once. She was to pay back the money over a period of several months, and she was to deliver the installments to him personally in his office each time.

"That was his way of making me face the truth about what I was doing," Diana said. "And he was right. I wasn't *taking*—I was *stealing*. I was robbing myself of my good opinion, my self-respect, too, and he was giving me a chance to earn them back."

I don't like to think of myself as someone who could deliberately do wrong . . . and yet I know there is that potential in me because I am human. Like the Quaker who saw a man going to the gallows and said, "There, but for the grace of God, go I." You and I cannot claim credit for the times we do not sin. The occasions are many and the temptations are powerful—much too powerful for us to resist. We need help. . . . As much as we tell ourselves that we could never do such things as we condemn in others, the truth is, we *can*. And we do. Whether our sins are large or small, monstrous or "human," seen or unseen, we commit them. It is our human condition—and on our own we aren't strong enough to do otherwise.

But Someone Else is . . . Someone Else can help us put another person's need before our own. . . . Someone Else can open our eyes to the fact that "everybody" may be wrong.

Colleen Townsend Evans

"I dreaded going to the manager's office that first time," Diana recalls. "I expected him to treat me like a criminal. Well, he didn't. He introduced me to the other people in the office as if I were a customer. He always thanked me. He would ask me about my family and my friends and my job. And he would tell me about his wife and daughter. We became friends, he and I. And when I brought in the last installment, we prayed together. For each other.

181

"I'm so glad I got caught, and by someone who really cared about me. That's why I tell this story to as many young people as I can get to listen. I want them to know that it *does* matter when you take something and don't pay for it. Or when you take something that doesn't belong to you. It matters to *you*. And you *know* it matters to God. Maybe nobody misses what you took. But *you* do—because you lose some part of yourself each time. That's what sin does to us. We stop trusting ourselves. Little by little I stole more things, bigger things, and I kept telling myself I wasn't being dishonest. Now—how can you love a person like that?

"I was lucky. That store manager gave me a chance to decide who I was going to be—a thief or a person I could trust with my life."

Prayer for the Reader

Jesus, don't let me settle for an excuse when I am tempted to take what isn't mine. There really isn't any excuse—and I think You made that very clear when You turned over all those tables in the temple.

WHEN A SPOUSE STARTS TO WORK

"God has given each of you some special abilities; be sure to use them to help each other."

(I Peter 4:10, Living Bible)

In this circumstance, the word *spouse* refers to a wife. Because when a husband starts to work, that's considered "normal." Even today, with so many married women working outside the home, many of us aren't comfortable with the idea. It seems to go against tradition.

> I sometimes wonder, Lord—is this work fair to my husband?
>
> He knows that I want to do it; he encourages me in it. And he helps so much—around the house, with the children, looking after so many things to make it easier for me.
>
> And that is partly the trouble. No matter how much I earn or contribute there is somehow this sense of guilt. Is it right that he do these things? Does it deplete his sense of masculinity somewhat?
>
> *Marjorie Holmes*

I remember how awkward I felt several years ago when I went on a business trip by myself for the first time. I was very excited about it, but something inside me kept telling me there was something wrong. A wife shouldn't go off and leave her husband to look after himself. Should she?

I had a few hours to myself one afternoon, and, being a history buff, I was delighted to learn that a restored Early American village was within walking distance. It was charming. And exactly what I needed!

Each house was not only a dwelling, but a vivid expression of each family member. Musical instruments in the parlor told me that the family enjoyed music, and the tiny simplified version of a violin meant that the children were included. A spinning wheel, larger than others I had seen, was used by a man. A father made the family's shoes at a bench in the parlor—not off in some basement by himself. His wife's knitting was in a cloth pocket of a small table; on top of it were some books.

And the kitchen? Not very large. Efficient is a better word to describe it. "Most of the roasting and baking was done in the local bakery ovens," our guide explained.

"But what did women *do*?" someone asked.

"They worked," the guide said. "They taught school. They gave music lessons. They worked in some of the shops—in sales and keeping accounts. Some of them ran their own businesses."

Well, that made all of us curious. Wasn't it unusual, we asked, for women to hold down jobs in that day and age?

No. Apparently the village was typical of colonial America. After breakfast an Early American family left their house at the same time—the children on their way to school, and both father and mother off to work. I don't believe anyone thought about roles in those days. There was work to be done—God gave you a gift and you used it.

And in the evening, when the family returned, if we can put together a picture from the things they left behind, they continued using their gifts to make life good. Dinner, music, handwork, prayer. And books! Many, many books.

I left the village when it was time to go back to a meeting. And—I felt quite normal. I still do.

> We all require room to breathe. When promising relationships suddenly blow apart, it is often because one partner was manipulated or boxed in.
>
> *Alan Loy McGinnis*

Prayer for the Reader

Sometimes I try to do too much, Lord, and that's when I run into problems. I get tired and impatient. I'm not a pleasant person to be around. Give me the wisdom to count on my family's love for me and ask them for help. My gifts need their gifts.

WHEN A PARENT IS GETTING OLD

"I have been young, and now am old...."

(Psalm 37:25, KJV)

You notice it in little ways, at first, so it's easy to persuade yourself it isn't happening. For instance, even with her glasses on, your mother has trouble reading the newspaper. But so do you. Sometimes. Going up and down stairs, slowly, tires your dad. More than it should. Or, more than you think it should. You make excuses for crankiness, forgetfulness, long gloomy staring instead of that wonderful smiling disposition. Nobody smiles all the time.

You tell yourself, No, it can't be—your parents aren't old. Why, they're still young by comparison. So are you.

It's hard for any of us to admit that a parent is getting old. The word itself sounds ugly. I know a sprightly man of almost seventy who is totally preoccupied with worry over the health of his mother, who must be near ninety—and who is, indeed, not well. This is a man who prided himself on keeping active, on being at his desk by eight o'clock every morning and putting in a full day's work. He was going to work until he died, he vowed. Now he stays home, helping his wife look after his frail mother.

I can remember the first time I looked at my mother and acknowledged, with a shock, that she was middle-aged. She had always seemed so young and full of energy. Her skin was without wrinkles and her hair without a trace of gray in it, at least, none that I could see. Then one day, all of a sudden, my mother looked different to me. We were riding a bus together and I turned to say something to her. Just then the sunlight coming through the window next to her illuminated what I hadn't seen before. Nothing much, really. A few tiny lines around her eyes and the corners of her mouth. Were they really *gray* hairs wisping at her temple? Or was it the sun playing games in her brown hair? I couldn't speak. I felt frightened, for some reason. I felt exactly the way my almost-seventy friend feels now.

The aging of parents tells us that someday we are going to be without them, and we don't want to be reminded of that. It hurts too much.

After two months, Mother came home but she never regained her strength. I nursed her, and did her cooking and cleaning, but she gradually went downhill.

. . . Ever since Dad's death, Mother had been trying to prepare me for the time when she, too, would die. "Now, Norma," she would say, "when I die, don't mourn for me like you did for your father. I'm ready to go. You've given me many years of happiness. I've had a good life since I came here. Be happy for me when I go." But I loved her too much. I couldn't bear the thought of losing her.

Norma Zimmer

It also reminds us that we too must move on, must face a diminishing of our strength and abilities. And somewhere deep inside us is the childlike conviction that a parent is the one person who stands between us and death. Once the parent is gone, we think we have lost that protection and we feel terribly mortal. We know now that we too must deal with death someday.

Does that seem morbid? It can be if we consider death the end of life. But as Christians we know it isn't. Death is a transition time for us. It *is* frightening to think about because we have never been there and we don't know what to expect—in human terms that is. Spiritually we have been well prepared— by the Parent Who will never leave us: God Himself.

I will never leave you nor forsake you.

(Hebrews 13:5, NKJV)

So old age becomes a preparation time for another part of life. It requires respect, not resignation.

Really to love is to listen. It is not so long since in some circles it was the custom to forbid children to speak at the table. The adults' conversation flowed around them, and they were unable to take part in it. The same thing still happens with old people. There are families in which both children and adults give noisy expression to their views, arguing and answering back over the heads of the old, who are given no opportunity to speak, because nobody bothers to think that they might have anything to say. They feel that they are looked upon as worn-out and of no further importance. Or else they are spoken to in a particular tone of voice, as used to be the case with the children, condescendingly, kindly, perhaps even affectionately, but in a way which indicates that no valid reply can be expected.

Paul Tournier

Not all parents are alike, so don't try to push your parents into a way of life that isn't comfortable for them. If they haven't been groupies, don't urge them to get into volunteer work. On the other hand, if they have always been the kind who love to start new projects, give them encouragement; they shouldn't stop now.

Somewhere along the way we will have to confront the problem of where will our parents live when they get too old to look after themselves. The answer will not be the same for all of us—or for all of them, and they should participate in the decision. Some families can deal with the elderly; some senior citizens can fit right into a multigenerational home. Some cannot, and there is nothing wrong with that distinction.

She scuttled through the house like a lost child, her air determined, but now more anxious for reassurance. One minute she seemed gone from us. The next, she astonished us with her perceptions. There were still times when she could fix me with an eye of such cold clarity I feared she saw straight into my soul.

...Four times during the summer she wandered from the house. Four times she was returned to me, her hand resting on a policeman's arm, a vague smile on her lips, a shade of trepidation in her eyes.

I never understood my mother's wanderings, whether she set off in search of something, or as an escape. One day she sat at her old, history-scarred Duncan Phyfe table and stared out the window, her mottled face resting in her hands, her white hair like a halo in the sunlight. "I think I'll go home now," she said, walked out the front door, inspected the garden, and came in the back.

It's easy to say the senile are like children, but they are not. They have been wounded too often. They've seen old friends grow tired and die. They've seen the young walk as if they, the elderly, did not exist. On some level, these things registered with Mother, and increased her apprehension.

In addition to her illness, it was stress, things others said or did, that threw her off. In recent years she no longer cooked, sewed, gardened, but out of mistaken kindness everyone maintained the fiction that she did. Too late we learned the gravity of our error in not maintaining reality, in taking away too much too soon. The elderly *need* daily tasks to perform, problems to solve. They need to abide by old disciplines. Encouragement, care, nutrition: all are important, but first comes a purpose for survival.

...At its core, the problem of caring for the elderly seems to split into three questions: What will make a person happiest? What is best for a person? What is best for the family? Often the answers are not the same.

Bonnie Ghazarbekian

A new experience in communal living had begun in November, 1977 when Peter and his family moved temporarily into the house next to ours in Florida.

At that time the family stretched all the way from Peter Jonathan, age three, and Mary Elizabeth, almost eight, to my mother, their great-grandmother, eighty-seven. Our plan had been to retain the two smaller family units for breakfasts and lunches but have communal evening meals, alternating between the two homes.

As time went on the dinner hour remained the reporting and clearing center for the day's events and for the thoughts, insights, and problems we wanted to share. Most of the time the dilemma was getting in a word edgewise. This proved especially frustrating to Peter Jonathan to whom we promised to set aside a chunk of time so that even his "news" could be heard.

Typically, Mary Elizabeth might report what she had learned in school that day about chlorophyll in leaves of plants and about the distributive property of multiplication.

Len was doing what he loves most: nurturing and building a Christian work from a small beginning.

Peter's book, written with David Manuel, *The Light and the Glory*, had sold 80,000 copies. . . .

That day ten eager women had come to my mother's weekly, home Bible study on the epistles of John.

Recreation was an important lubricant for this extended family life. Such fun as Peter teaching Peter Jonathan how to throw a ball and swing a baseball bat; swimming lessons; handicrafts; Peter Jonathan and Mary Elizabeth learning correct tennis from their grandfather Len; family tennis doubles; Peter Jonathan and Mary Elizabeth cuddled up to Len, one on each side of him, listening spellbound to one of their grandfather's "Lucky stories."

Lucky stories are now family tradition, wild tales of suspense, always in exotic settings, with a man named "Lucky" as the hero, the story always containing a moral.

Then, as in all extended families, there are those special affinities that develop person to person. What *is* that special bond between Peter Jonathan and his great-grandmother "Nana"? Who can tell! Is it that age has dropped out a lot of false values and finally retains the imperishables—a childlike imagination and faith?

There are many pluses and blessings for extended families such as ours has been for the three-and-a-half-year period. Among them, the obvious advantage of always having someone around for baby-sitting and child care; always someone to read or tell stories to the children or to play games; always someone for the mending and the darning, for the household baking or to prepare vegetables for dinner, to make special desserts, even perhaps a big freezer of homemade peach or strawberry ice cream.

When I was growing up, it was a usual thing for families to include a grandparent, an uncle or aunt, or an unmarried daughter or a bachelor son.

The change in family life today is startling. Now not only is the extended family a rarity; even the intact nuclear family is becoming the exception.

Behind all this is a rampant "me-first" philosophy. Endlessly, we are hearing about the "rights of the individual." The question then becomes, does solitary, self-centered living really enable one to find oneself? Does selfishness bring happiness and fulfillment?

Our experiment in communal living has shed much light on these crucial questions, for four generations cannot live together without rubbings. In that lovely verse from the Psalms, we are told that "God sets the solitary in families." Now we know why: He knows, if we do not, that every husband and every wife are "incompatible"; all parents are "incompatible" with all children. So what does that prove? Only that the Creator made each human being a distinctly unique individual.

So we found it. The rubbing and scraping often produced a crisis. God's way is not to flee the crisis but to uncover the root of it and so a growing edge of the inner spirit. As we handled problems together in prayer, we surrendered yet another layer of selfishness and subsequently grew in maturity.

For instance, my mother frantically called to Edith one afternoon, "Quick! Get Peter Jonathan down. He's climbed almost to the top of the big mango tree."

Edith's response was calm. "Gram, it's all right for him to climb trees."

We were learning that the same "Christy" who, at 19, traveled alone into the Great Smokies, walked seven miles through the snow with the mailman to get to Cutter's Gap, was a daring horse-woman, and faced down moonshiners, now approaching 90—has many fears as she looks about her at our world.

That night at dinner the heart of the question was submitted: How many of my mother's fears were the wisdom of age and therefore legitimate? Or could we be in danger of passing on to children a fear-filled attitude to life?

The discussion grew heated. The woman who so many years

before had swept majestically into Mr. Rush Hazen's office, flaunting her big-plumed hat, the same one who had stood off the roughest mountaineers, can still be fiery: she could not help her fears for the children's safety and thought them legitimate.

"But," Edith protested, "it isn't that I want any life-threatening danger for my child...."

"Isn't falling out of a high tree life-threatening?" Mother shot back, sparks in her eyes.

"I want my son to have the freedom to climb and run, to have some rough and tumble," Peter interjected. "Children, especially boys, can't be protected from all danger and hurt, Grandmother."

Almost always our give-and-take sessions end up in prayer for the wisdom of God's specific direction for the problem and for the right attitude in each of us. For throughout these years we have found prayer the best lubricant of all—in fact, indispensable.

As in all families, selfishness, jealousy, haughtiness, anger erupt at times. If it comes from a child, then there is a correction; if from an adult, we gather together to pray it through, letting the Helper—the Holy Spirit—do the correcting. It is amazing how often He does, with gentle incisiveness.

Catherine Marshall

What is right, and what is important, is for all of us to remember that no matter what a person's age, he or she is still a unique individual made in the image of God—and still growing! Physically, and sometimes even mentally, we all slow down as the years go by, but we can continue to develop the special abilities God has given us. Should we do it in a community of our peers in age? Or in a family that sometimes crackles with the tensions that must arise between generations with different lifestyles? This is a decision each of us must be allowed to make in consultation with God.

Prayer for the Reader

Lord, help me to grow up a little more as I see my parents aging. It's a difficult time for them—and for me. I need to let go of them just enough so that they are free to move closer to You, but not so much that they feel I have abandoned them. Let me be someone they can lean on when they need strength—but let me also be a grateful recipient of the support they can still provide. I need it, Lord. Let us be leaners, each on the other.

BEING LOYAL

"I have loved thee with an everlasting love...."

(Jeremiah 31:3, KJV)

Loyalty is tunnel vision. It is seeing only what one wants to see—one's commitment to another, one's concern for the other's well-being. It is an absolute blindness to opportunities to hurt, betray, deceive.

Loyalty is not popular. It isn't flexible. It is unbelievably stubborn. It makes up its own mind. It has its own values. It is irritatingly patient. It speaks up, in both praise and protest. It is extremely sensitive and can see what is not always evident, hear what is not always spoken.

Loyalty doesn't get carried away with emotion, but it feels life deeply. It loves hard; in fact, it refuses to stop loving even when it is not loved back.

Loyalty can suffer terribly. It can be crucified by temptation for persisting in its love, and it will not die. It will, in its agony, bless what it loves.

Affection is delightful. It insists that we love and makes loving easy. But loyalty is choosing to love. It is one of those difficult freedoms that gives more than it gets.

> God, through the angel Gabriel, called on Mary to do what, in the world's eyes, is impossible, and instead of saying, "I can't," she replied immediately, "Be it unto me according to thy Word."
>
> God is always calling on us to do the impossible. It helps me to remember that anything Jesus did during his life here on earth is something we should be able to do, too.
>
> *Madeleine L'Engle*

Prayer for the Reader

Lord, give me Your determined, feet-on-the-ground kind of love. I want something that lasts.

WHEN A MARRIAGE ENDS

"Let my cry come before You, O Lord;
Give me understanding according to Your word."

(Psalm 119:169, NKJV)

It doesn't seem possible that love can die, does it? You remember the vows and the way you felt when you spoke them. *Forever* was something you could feel.

Once a woman phoned me and told me how her life had just exploded around her. She explained she'd just learned her husband had affairs with five of her best friends over a period of several years. That was the good-news part of her phone call. The bad news was, "He is a minister, and all of the women are in his congregation."

I wish it were true that good Christian husbands are not deserting their wives and children, but the facts, here again, just aren't so. Desertion is probably the best kept secret in the world of marriage breakdowns, but this year an estimated one hundred thousand men will leave their wives, families, and homes. For the first time in our history, the number of women leaving their homes by desertion will be almost even with the men's percentage, so the problem is not limited to men.

...The break-up in the home, the moral decay, the loss of love in relationships are huge puzzles. Puzzling us the most, however, is a marriage that looks sound, solid, and seems to be moving in a meaningful way; yet one day, out of the blue, it splinters into a thousand pieces before our eyes.

Joyce Landorf

Whoever was at fault, whoever changed, whoever ended it, that's all over. You will have to confront the memories, the shame, anger and sense of failure, but not now. There is something else you have to do first: Think about your life.

Yes, your life. It must go on. Not as it was before. Not even the way it was before you married. This is all new. All different. All very frightening.

194

You have had a death in the family. No, let me put it another way. There's been a death *of* a family—a particular family. And you grieve.

With a death in the family there are rituals to perform that can help you overcome grief. Friends come to call. You have arrangements to make, hymns to sing, Scripture to read. There's a funeral.

There is no funeral for the death of a marriage. Yet you grieve.

. . .The end of a marriage, whether it was a good one or a rotten one, raises feelings of self-doubt, questions about your worth as an individual. Dependent people measure themselves by their relationships. When there is none, they have lost their measuring stick. The questions come and you have only yourself to answer. *Why did this happen to me? Could I have prevented it? How can I go on? Where did I go wrong? What's wrong with me?*

Marilyn Jensen

You grieve differently from other people—not so differently that you cannot find fellowship in suffering with them, yet so differently that no one else's grief is exactly like your own.

Wayne E. Oates

But the hurt—what about that? Blows have been exchanged. Wounds inflicted. Pride crushed. All the love, all the care, all the softness you once felt is gone. You're hard, flinty. You've become a weapon poised to strike back.

Is that what you want? Forget about what is fair and what is right. Do you want to worship the god of vengeance? Or the God of love? Do you want to be guided by hate or by compassion? Take your choice.

God isn't going to force you to do anything. If you want to get even, you can justify it. You have your reasons. If you want to spend a good part of your life inflicting pain on someone else, you have that freedom. But you're cutting yourself off from God. Oh, He's on your side. He always will be. But He can't act in hate. He acts in love.

You know what love is. Once, perhaps for a long time, you felt love for the person you now hate. You cared what happened in that person's life. You felt everything he or she experienced as if it happened to you. That won't change. Not entirely. You will feel the pain from any wounds you cause now. Because love doesn't die, even though a relationship may. A part of love remains in you and in the person who shared your life. A small ember of love, perhaps. A bit of regard. But it will always be there. God did join the two of you together, and nothing on earth can totally separate you.

If Jesus of Nazareth was God become truly man for us, as I believe He was, then we should be able to walk on water, to heal the sick, even to accept the Father's answer to our prayers when it is not the answer that we hope for, when it is *No*. Jesus begged in anguish that He be spared the bitter cup, and then humbly added, "but not as I will, Father; as you will."

Madeleine L'Engle

Let kindness be what remains. Let kindness be what you eventually remember long after you rebuild your life. Let kindness be what you take with you. God can help you do that.

Prayer for the Reader

O merciful Father, help me to realize that I am not really a failure. I feel that there is nothing lovable in me. Can You teach me how to care for and love what You have made? You know how—and I want to learn.

REACHING BEYOND OUR LIMITS:
Serving Out of Answered Need

God gives us His spiritual power to grow in goodness....

WHEN YOU'RE ANGRY AT SOMEONE YOU LOVE

"If you are angry, don't sin by nursing your grudge. Don't let the sun go down with you still angry—get over it quickly."

(Ephesians 4:26, Living Bible)

We prefer to believe that Jesus never lost His temper with someone who was close to Him. How easily we forget His outbursts at Peter, Thomas, Martha, and even Mary, His mother. We really don't like to be reminded that real love isn't always tranquil. And no wonder. When a relationship, especially a close one, is torn by conflicting emotions, we are thrown into confusion. Is there something wrong with us? If we love someone, how can we possibly hate the person? Even for a few minutes?

Remember that you can love and be angry at the same time. Most of us have a certain mixture of love and anger in all our intimate relationships, and if you will remind yourself of that fact as your loved one is railing, it may help.

Alan Loy McGinnis

Loving someone doesn't mean we love everything about the person. And no matter how carefully we try to avoid areas of conflict, we must, at times, deal with them. The longer we put off the confrontation, the more difficult it will be. We owe ourselves, and the person we love/hate a Christlike openness.

Families need some way to reach out to one another with love and forgiveness. Most of us haven't had much experience with true forgiveness. We need to learn how to ask for, grant, and accept forgiveness.

Where do you start when your spouse makes fun of you in public? When you've jumped on your kids for something petty? When your mother flies off the handle? When your daughter is caught shoplifting? When you and your brother have a big argument? When your partner turns away from your request for lovemaking? How do you give and receive forgiveness in the family?

The starting point is to acknowledge that forgiveness is not a feeling—it's a choice. It's actually two choices—the decision made by one person to repent and the decision made by the other to forgive. When you've done something for which you need forgiveness, admit it. Swallow your pride, take the risk, and make your request directly to the injured person: "Steve, will you forgive me? I really hurt you, and I'm sorry." This kind of direct request gives the other person the chance to say, "Yes, I forgive you," rather than retaliate. It also provides a wonderful model for others in the family to imitate.

When others wrong you, choose to forgive them as God has freely forgiven you. If you can let go of your righteous indignation when you've been hurt, you'll go a long way toward bringing the forgiveness factor to life in your family.

Forgiveness is not forgetting; it's refusing to hold grudges. Forgiveness is an attitude freely given that accepts hurts and drops the charges.

Donald A. Tubesing and Nancy Loving Tubesing

There may be days when disagreements and disturbing emotions may come between us. There may be times when psychological or physical miles may lie between us. But I have given you the word of my commitment. I have set my life on a course. I will not go back on my word to you. So feel free to be yourself, to tell me of your negative and positive reactions, of your warm and cold feelings. I cannot always predict my reactions or guarantee my strength, but one thing I do know and I do want you to know: I will not reject you! I am committed to your growth and happiness. I will always love you.

John Powell

Sometimes openness will not be enough. If you have ever been wounded by a friend's anger, then you know how long it takes for the wound to heal.

A few years ago my friend Mark Svensson ripped into me something fierce. He thought I was committing a major blunder, acting stupidly, and letting him and some other people down. I sat in the car and took it, but was I mad! He was completely off base, he didn't appreciate why I had made the decision, and he was a poor friend to be so critical.

I went home mad and the next day I was still mad. I canceled our regular Tuesday lunch because I was so mad. Wednesday Mark called to see how I was. I was icy in my replies, clipped in my responses. I was still smarting from my wounds.

Mark knew he had angered me, yet he felt he had no occasion to apologize. What he did on the telephone that day, in person the next evening, and consistently for a number of days thereafter until I was through pouting, was to express his affection for me. He had been genuinely indignant at what I had done, he had told me so clearly and was glad he had, yet he knew that it had hurt me, and he understood my being miffed. It did not take many days of his affectionate displays for me to forget the whole thing.

I learned an important lesson from Mark then. It was this: You can get away with many expressions of anger if you balance them with lots of expressions of love.

Alan Loy McGinnis

The question is, how can we express our anger without destroying our love?

Two people who have earned the respect of each other have the right to have a kind, loving, open honesty with one another. This vehicle makes it possible for them to work out the conflicts of their hearts. The key to nonabusive language, though, is making sure you discuss the problem. Do not attack the person, because all that does is destroy his feelings of self-worth. When he sees his self-image being destroyed, he becomes hostile and defensive. Then all you've got is a rip-roaring argument with both parties flailing away at each other in hot anger. Stick with the issue at hand (don't confuse this issue by digging up old issues, either) and leave out the personalities as much as possible.

Joyce Landorf

There are times when anger can't be expressed to a spouse. God will be the only recipient of that anger expression (through confession). Possibly the spouse is too threatened to be able to handle it at that time. Or, we're endeavoring to break a pattern of always spewing anger. Consequently, anger is directed to God: "Father, I'm angry." The circumstances can be elaborated. "God, forgive me. Change me. You are my forgiving, loving Saviour who can give me a loving spirit for that person."

Then you can go to the partner and say, "You know, I've just gone through a tough time. I've been on my knees and have dealt with my reaction of anger. But your forgetting my birthday today really hurt me. I was very angry about it. I want you to know my feelings, because I know that you want us to have a growing marriage relationship."

Notice the dynamics here. The person has faced, expressed, and resolved the anger within. There was no build-up of destructive physical, psychological, or spiritual symptoms. Communication continued with the partner, building an open and growing relationship. This allows no chance for anyone to become a doormat.

Ray Burwick

Prayer for the Reader

Dear Lord, why am I trying to be so perfect when, quite clearly, I am not? And why do I expect my loved ones to be without fault? If I am under the impression that love can exist only where there are no faults, then I am certainly forgetting how You love us. I need to remember. Always.

GROWING OLD

"Even in old age they will still produce fruit and be vital and green. This honors the Lord, and exhibits his faithful care."

(Psalm 92:14–15, Living Bible)

When I showed up for lunch, Mrs. Baxter wasn't home and her housekeeper wasn't expecting me. I was embarrassed. Did I get my dates mixed up?

No, the housekeeper said, probably Mrs. Baxter did. "When you're ninety-six," she said, "I guess you're entitled to forget a few things, don't you think?"

I agreed. And when Mrs. Baxter called that afternoon to apologize, I was delighted that she asked me to come for lunch the next day.

It was a wonderful occasion. Emily Baxter's home was filled with fine old furniture handed down through her family from generation to generation. She knew when and why and by whom each piece had been made, and she was a good storyteller. The house itself had been built and lived in by a signer of the Declaration of Independence, one of her forebears.

Two other guests were there, an elderly couple who had just delivered some of Mrs. Baxter's old books which they had rebound in leather, matching the gold tooling with that of the original. I didn't know anyone rebound books in leather these days, I commented. Very few people could, the couple told me, which is why they had all the business they could handle. I was fascinated, listening to them describe how they were able to give new life to a rare old book that couldn't possibly be duplicated today.

Some people seem to resent the fact that they are growing old. They hide their age in every possible way. Yet it would be a lot worse if, instead of older, we were steadily getting younger.

Just suppose the process were reversed. You would start living at an old age and every day be a little younger. Now that would be terrible. Every day you would know a little less than you knew the day before. You would start off with your grandchildren, but in a few years they would all be gone. Your family, instead of growing, would constantly be diminishing. You would eventually get to the age when you start to college. You would start off a senior and end up in the first grade. Now, little first graders are cute with their short pants or little pink dresses, but I would hate to think I would have to be one again.

Tottering old age has its drawbacks, but being a tiny baby is a lot worse. If you were getting younger, you would have to look forward to losing everything and end up by being a helpless baby with a bottle. Finally, you would just fade away into nothing. Babies do not have a previous existence, so complete oblivion would be the end.

Charles L. Allen

My grandmother's hands were terribly crippled by arthritis. She would tell me they hurt—when I asked. However, almost to the year of her death, she kept a spotless house, took meticulous care of her yard *and* garden, and walked to the neighborhood store for her own groceries nearly every day. She never became a mean ole lady, even though she was widowed, deaf, and crippled with painful arthritis. She replaced criticism and complaints with thankful praise.

Joyce Landorf

Speaking of fine old treasures, we went on to the subject of the national tour of artifacts recovered from King Tut's tomb. Had anyone seen the exhibit? I asked.

Before the others could answer, Mrs. Baxter corrected me. It was Tutankhamen, not Tut, she said. And then she went on to describe the ancient Egyptian collection in detail. I had seen the exhibit, but, hearing about it from her, I knew I had missed a lot. Of course, she explained, she was speaking from memory, and she might have forgotten a few pieces. You see, she had been in Egypt on vacation when the tomb was discovered, and she had seen the contents when they were first displayed in Cairo. She had talked with Carter and Carnarvon, the two archeologists who became famous for finding the tomb, which had been carefully hidden thousands of years ago.

I had studied about Tutankhamen's tomb when I was in college—and that was a *long* time ago. The tomb had been discovered in the early 1920's and it was doubtful that anyone connected with the event was still alive. *But Mrs. Baxter had been there!* She could see the excavation from her hotel. She could remember and describe it to us in a way no historian could match, and we all sat spellbound.

By then she was tired and it was time for her guests to leave. Reluctantly.

She leaned heavily on her cane as she took us to the door. Then she remembered something she wanted to show me. "You're interested in books, so you'll like this," she said, leading me into a small room off the hallway. She picked up a cassette from a pile next to a tape player on a table.

"I can't see well enough to read any more," she said, "and they tell me my eyes are too old for glasses, so this is my new pair of eyes." The cassette was a reading from the Bible. "You'd be surprised how many good books are on tape nowadays," she said. "I read my magazines and newspapers that way, too. I like to keep up with what's going on."

I loved being a grandmother. Not since I was a small girl had I had so much fun. Not only that, I learned volumes about the delight of living in the Kingdom of God while still on this earth.

As a tiny girl Mary Elizabeth had large, round blue eyes and a piquant nose framed by blonde hair like her mother's. By the time she could walk, she had sturdy, well-formed legs that carried her into the most unlikely places, a disarming smile with a touch of coyness, and a way of pronouncing "Yes" and "Oh, no—no—*no*" that made her sound like a charter member of the Women's Liberation Movement.

When this child visited us what she did to our household was remarkable. My writing schedule was forgotten while Mary Elizabeth and I would enjoy a tea party using tiny blue cups which I had carted from Salzburg, Austria, in anticipation of such a golden moment. Our son Jeffrey had no objection to

204

becoming a baby tender. He never walked Mary Elizabeth around the block in her stroller; he raced her while she chortled. And when she flirted with her grandfather, Len would become so entranced he would drop down on all fours, bray like a donkey and kick his heels in the air.

All of this added up to joy.

Catherine Marshall

Having achieved ninety-three birthdays in this early life, I wish to say that the older we grow the more we realize that life is worth the living. We think too little of the fun there is in it; we are too parsimonious of laughter. The secret of happiness and longevity, in my judgment, is to cherish and cultivate cheerful, hopeful, buoyant spirits. If you haven't them, create them! Let us never lose our faith in human nature, no matter how often we may be deceived. Do not let such deceptions destroy confidence in the real honest goodness, generosity, humanity and friendship that exist in the world. Believe me, they are overwhelmingly in the majority.

Chauncey M. Depew

Going home that day, I knew that Mrs. Baxter herself was a rare and fine old treasure. She had shown us how the past becomes part of the present through her awareness of the special qualities of each. She had gifted us with a sense of ongoing life, and out of that came a new appreciation of God's endless creation.

Mrs. Baxter always said she wanted to live to be one hundred. She didn't make it. She died when she was ninety-seven. She was listening to a new best-seller on tape when she just seemed to go to sleep. A few days earlier she had said she thought the Lord was ready for her. And she always trusted His judgment.

I miss her. But I still have her with me in the memories she bequeathed to me.

Prayer for the Reader

Is there a place for me, Lord, in this youth-minded world? Is there something of value in me that I can give to the young? Am I too proud to see that they have something for me? Help us to pass life on to one another.

WHEN A FRIEND HAS HURT YOU

"This friend of mine betrayed me—I who was at peace with him. He broke his promises."

(Psalm 55:20, Living Bible)

The pain was even more excruciating because I didn't see it coming. I didn't expect it from a friend.

At first I couldn't believe my friend would do such a thing. But eventually I had to face the truth. Someone I trusted betrayed me.

I felt more than pain. I felt rejected, as if somehow I was of no value. For a time I was angry and wanted to strike back. *How could she do this to me!* Then I began to think it might have been my fault. Not that I had done anything to provoke my friend, but rather that I was simply not worth cherishing. I admired my friend and thought she admired me. Obviously I was wrong. She thought nothing of me. And perhaps I was not someone to be admired.

Do you see where I was headed?

There is no situation that cannot be healed. Love has staying power.

Earl F. Palmer

Only one love has staying power, and that is the love of God. Only one Person will put us first and even die for us, and that is Jesus Christ. We cannot expect even a reasonable facsimile of that love from ourselves—or from anyone else. We do the best we can, but we fall far short of the mark.

Yes, a friend can hurt us. And we can hurt our friends—sometimes without realizing it, at other times with malice intended. The question is, can the friendship survive the wounds? Does our human love have any staying power at all?

207

If we are to forgive freely, we need a tolerance of others as generous as that tolerance we display toward our own errors. It is remarkable how understanding we can be of our own flops in interpersonal dealings—we didn't intend the error, or it happened in a moment of stress, or we weren't feeling right that day, or we'll know better next time. We tend to see ourselves not for what we are but for what we strive to be, whereas we see others for what they are. Jesus, in his encounters with people such as Peter and the woman at the well, saw them for what they could be. To extend such understanding toward our intimates can do a great deal to build strong friendships.

Alan Loy McGinnis

It isn't fair to call upon a friend to make us feel whole. To make us feel accepted and loved. It isn't fair to love someone with any expectation of being loved in return. That isn't love; it's bartering. And when the other person can't give something in return, the deal is off. The friendship is over.

Can we love a friend in spite of the hurt? Not that we must turn our eyes away from the incident. Not that we must resume the friendship only on the condition that we will never be hurt again. Be assured, the wounding will happen again. Can we take it and still love the one who did it?

We can try.

A girl I'll call Sandra phoned several months ago to tell me that she had just been asked to be godmother to her friend Vicky's child. It was impossible, Sandra said, to consider such a thing since Vicky, once a close friend, had hurt her very deeply. The two couples had vacationed together and their friendship disintegrated over a series of trivial but unforgivable hurts. They had hardly seen each other since, and now here was Vicky expecting Sandra to be her child's godmother. What was Sandra to do?

"Forgive her," I said.

"Forgive her! But she isn't even sorry. I don't think she even remembers how she hurt me!"

Nevertheless, I told her, if it was her Christian duty she was asking me about, there was no question as to what it was.

"You mean I'm the one who has to make the move?"

"Do you expect God to forgive you for your sins?"

"Well, certainly."

"Then you must forgive Vicky."

"Is there someplace in the Bible that actually *says* that?"

"Remember the Lord's Prayer? 'Forgive us our trespasses as we forgive those who trespass against us.' That's followed by a pretty plain statement: 'If you do not forgive men their trespasses, neither will your Father forgive you your trespasses.' "

I could almost hear Sandra catch her breath on the telephone. There was a pause.

"I never thought of that. And I said that prayer just this morning. So. . .I can't expect to be forgiven unless I forgive?"

She didn't see how she could do that. I agreed most emphatically that she could not—not without God's grace. Everything in human nature goes against that idea. But the Gospel is the message of *reconciliation*. Reconciliation not only to God, but to his purposes in the world, and to all our fellow human beings. We talked for a little while about the absolute necessity of forgiveness. It is a command. It is the road to restoration of ruptured friendships. It releases us from ourselves. I promised Sandra I would pray for the grace of God to work in her and in Vicky, and that she would be enabled freely and completely to forgive.

"But what if she still isn't sorry?"

"We don't pray, 'Forgive us our trespasses as we forgive those who ask us to.' We say 'as we forgive those who trespass against us.' It's not a matter of *ignoring* what's been done. When God forgives he doesn't merely overlook our trespasses. He doesn't ask us to overlook others' trespasses either—he asks us to forgive them. So that means our Christian obligation is to forgive anybody who has invaded our rights, our territory, our comfort, our self-image, whether they acknowledge the invasion or not."

A week later I learned that Sandra's and my prayers had been answered far beyond what either of us had had faith to expect. Not only did Sandra forgive, but Vicky even apologized, and the two were reconciled.

Elisabeth Elliot

I have known such reconciliations to strengthen a friendship. Once, when a serious disagreement threatened to sever the bond between a very dear person and me, I went through days of agony, some of it from the hurt I suffered, but much more of it from my realization that I loved my friend in spite of the dispute. I knew I would be losing someone valuable in my life if she went out of it. So I decided to fight—not to fight my friend, but to fight *for* the friendship, because the friendship suddenly became more important than the bruised feelings of either one of us. I kept telephoning her, trying to arrange reasons for us to meet. She kept finding reasons to avoid me. Finally unexpectedly, we met at another friend's house. I began awkwardly, but that lasted only seconds. I was overcome—not with memories of the hurt we had experienced, but by the love and regard I still felt for my friend. Apparently she was discovering the same thing. We held onto each other's hands for dear life and then hugged each other. Later, knowing that our friendship could survive the dispute, we were able to talk about it. And do you know what came of it? Interesting—after all the years we had known each other, we were at last able to accept the fact that we were entitled to our own opinions. Since then we have known a wonderful new sense of freedom in our relationship. We don't have to argue. We have the right to disagree.

But—reconciliation doesn't always happen, does it?

My heart was pounding in my throat as I began to tell her that I was aware of her attitude toward me. I recalled some of the hurtful remarks that had come back to me from others—and the jibes and digs I had heard and had been unable to forget. It felt so good to talk about them, to get them out into the open.

. . .She heard me out. Then, looking puzzled, she shook her head. "I really don't know what you're talking about," she said. "You and I have never been at odds."

. . ."As far as I know," she went on, "there is nothing for us to discuss."

. . .I felt sick. My approach had been rejected. . .And yet, I had felt so *led* to go to her. Surely the Holy Spirit knew what he was doing! Or had I misinterpreted him somewhere along the way?

I kept asking myself all those questions—over and over—

until the wee hours of the morning. It was then I heard the voice that was not a voice saying, "Whether she accepts your attempt at reconciliation is not your responsibility. . . . Forgive her for *not* forgiving." And with God's help, that is what I did. Only then did I sleep.

When I awoke later that morning I was tired—but free! No longer did I feel compelled to please this woman or go out of my way to prove I was worthy of her friendship. I loved her—she didn't have to feel that way. Love doesn't always win, but being able to love is what counts.

Colleen Townsend Evans

If dialogue fails, what do we do? We search for the reasons. Perhaps we were at fault. . . . *How* we say things can make all the difference in the world. Or it could be that the other person was hampered by pride, fear, or some other human fault. People resist change in their lives.

Then, what do we do? We learn from Jesus. He wanted harmony, but he did not want peace at any cost. He rocked the boat when this became necessary. Ask the Pharisees whom he confronted. Ask the money-changers who were driven out of the temple. So, too, a parent, a wife, a husband, an engaged person, a nun, a priest, a teacher, a boss—each one may very well have to take similar steps in a difficult situation. Then, it is hoped, the other person will return to the bargaining table.

Andrew Costello

Prayer for the Reader

O Lord, I try to love as You do, and I don't always succeed. Will You make up the difference? If I cannot love the person who hurts me, will You do the loving for me? And if my friend can no longer love me, teach me how to love from a distance, as You often have to do with us.

WHEN SOMEONE YOU TRUST DECEIVES YOU

"His words were softer than oil,
Yet they were drawn swords."

(Psalm 55:21, NKJV)

This is not the same as being hurt by a friend. It is not an accidental slight, a careless nick that stings. Deceit is deliberate. The wound you suffered was intentional.

And you are very, *very* angry.

You want to strike back, hurt for hurt. You feel your pulse drumming in your temples and your face is hot, the skin over your cheeks tingling—almost as if you had been slapped. Hard.

Well, you were. There is no denying that some wrong was done you. There is no excusing it. It happened. Someone you have known to be reliable in many ways turns out to be totally untrustworthy in others. You don't like to believe people behave that way. But they do. Some of them are more than imperfect; they are downright dangerous to be around. Not only can they harm you directly, but they can make you bring harm to yourself if you allow them.

Some years ago a friend of a friend asked me to help her write a book. She had done the research but had no idea how to organize it. The woman was very well regarded and I liked her; she was so open, so eager to turn out a good book. We agreed that I would help her make up a detailed outline of the book and write a few sample chapters based on her research. Fine. As an editor, I do that all the time. No need for anything in writing. We were two Christians who trusted each other. If a publisher wanted to publish the book, we would finish it and share the income from it.

I finished the outline and the chapters, and sent them off to my co-author. I never heard from her again. About a year and a half later, her book came out. It clearly followed the outline I had written, and, with the exception of a few words here and there, my sample chapters were included.

I was furious. I had heard of such things happening to other writers—but I *trusted* the woman! She allowed me to trust her. And then she deceived me. Had she planned to do that all along?

"Forget it, get on with your life," my friends advised me. I couldn't. My rage grew until I began to worry about what I might do if I ever saw the woman again. As I was driving along a busy street I would imagine seeing her step off the curb to cross in front of me—and in my fantasy I would roar ahead trying to run her down. I never finished those scenes, not even in my mind. I was too afraid of them. I never would have believed that I was capable of doing anyone such harm. Would I—if I had the chance? I was horrified at the thought that there was evil in me.

The sin is not in the coming of the thought, it is in the holding of it, the harboring of it. Thoughts of sin become sinful thoughts only when they are held and harbored.

E. Stanley Jones

I talked with a friend who is a psychiatrist. "I feel so guilty, I can't even ask God to help me," I told her. "What must He think of me?"

"Well, I'm sure He's very concerned," my friend said. "And I'm also sure He doesn't expect you to pretend you don't have these feelings. But just because you have them, that doesn't mean you have to act on them."

"What do you mean?" I asked. "I actually *hate* that woman! How can God forgive that?"

"He's dealt with hate before. He can forgive it—but can *you*? As long as you hold onto your hate, you belong to it. You are its prisoner. That's why you can't talk to God about it."

"What can I do to get free?" I said. I was crying, poking around in my bag for a tissue.

"You can get your hate out of your system in a perfectly harmless way," she said, "although it may sound a little silly to you when I describe it."

"Tell me!"

"You'll have to use your imagination, but in a more constructive way. You might try writing a story and using this woman as one of the characters in it. Then you can do anything you want with her and you won't be hurting

213

her. Write the story for yourself. Or don't even write it—just imagine it. And try to think of something funny you might arrange to happen to her—something that might make her feel foolish without doing her any real harm. And once *you* start to laugh, that's the end of your hate."

"But she'll never know!" I protested. "She'll never have to pay for what she did."

"That's not up to you, and you know that, my friend," she said. "Nobody was ever more deceived than Jesus was by Judas—and Judas did it with a kiss. And do you remember what Jesus said about Judas' treachery? 'Oh, the misery ahead for the man by whom I am betrayed. Oh, that he had never been born!' [Mark 14:21, Living Bible]. He wasn't asking God to do something terrible to Judas. But He trusted God to deal with the man in a way that was just—and He understood how deceit eats away at a person. He had compassion for Judas. Now, can't you do as much?"

I wasn't sure, but I knew I owed it to God and myself to try. I went home and sat down at my typewriter—and got nowhere. Talk about writer's block! If I couldn't invent something frightful to happen to the woman I hated, I couldn't write a word about her—until . . . .

I went downstairs to make dinner, more out of habit than appetite. Since I didn't feel like cooking, I began pulling leftovers out of the refrigerator. I cut them up, put them in a bowl and poured salad dressing over it all. And as I was tossing, I got the most wonderful idea. I imagined my nemesis sitting with friends at a table in a restaurant, dressed impeccably and ready to enjoy a lovely meal. A waiter came dashing out of the kitchen, a bowl of salad in each hand, and as he passed behind the woman's chair his arm was jostled by another waiter hurrying past. Up went a bowl of tossed salad and down it came on the woman's head—dressing and all. And I stood there, watching the scene taking place in my mind, not missing a single detail of the mess the salad made, and laughed. I thought I would never stop laughing. I was still grinning when I offered a prayer of thanks to God for removing my hate—for it was surely gone. I could, then, turn the breaking of a trust over to God and even offer an earnest prayer for His mercy—on both the woman I had hated and me.

What is it about Christian love that makes it able to stay and get to work on our crises, our sins, and our ethical problems? Agape love is able to come face to face with both the victims of sin and the perpetrators of sin because it sees a way through. It sees a way through human sin and human need because it believes in repentance and in redemption. That is why it can be reality oriented. That is why it doesn't have to run away from tragedy.

Earl F. Palmer

It is when our hearts are truly emptied out, wounded, made vulnerable, that we are able to receive the true comfort which comes from God himself, from his loving presence.

Luke Timothy Johnson

But—what about reconciliation? Can we ever resume a relationship with someone who has done us so much harm?

Sometimes.

It can be transforming to pray, "Father, forgive us our trespasses as we forgive those who trespass against us." A stockbroker, whom I will call George, tells about having a falling-out with another broker in the same office. They had a dispute over a customer, and after that, though they passed each other's desks every day, they did not speak. One day in church, as George was praying the Lord's Prayer, he came to that line on forgiveness. "There was no question in my mind," he says, "who was in the wrong. *Sam* had been in the wrong when he took my customer away from me. But it wasn't right for us not to be speaking, and I had to do something. While the others were repeating the rest of the prayer, I asked God to help me with Sam. On Monday afternoon, when the market had closed and I was finishing up some papers, I breathed another prayer and went over to Sam's desk and said, 'You know, Sam, you used to tell me about the trouble your wife was having with arthritis, and I've been wondering how she's getting along.'

"Sam looked startled at first, but then words began to tumble out—how they'd had her to three specialists in the past year, and that she was a little better, thank you. And as we talked he told about taking a walk together for two blocks the night before, which was pretty good. And among other things, he said that he was too quick with his tongue and often did things he didn't mean to do. Though he didn't come out and say it, I knew that was Sam's way of apologizing.

"And the next morning when he came by my desk, he said, just like he used to, 'Good morning, George!' And I said, just like I used to, 'Good morning, Sam!' "

Alan Loy McGinnis

And sometimes even when the person is long gone from our lives.

It's a matter of attitude. We can recognize the other person as someone of worth—he or she is someone God loves, someone for whom Christ died, and therefore a person of value.

Until recently Belinda found it impossible to forgive her father for the terrible shame he had brought to her life. She was very young when it happened, and until that time she had adored her father. They had been very close, and Belinda felt a special responsibility to bring cheer to her father's eyes when he was sad. And he was often sad, for there were many problems in the man's life. . . .One day, in a moment of deep anguish, he forced his daughter into an incestuous relationship, one that continued for the next few years until Belinda was able to leave home. She married, hastily and regrettably. Within a few years she was divorced and living alone, assaulted this time by the memories of her hatred for her father.

Belinda married again. Her husband is a patient, understanding man who has been very supportive to her. Gradually she felt she could trust people—life—again. The only obstacle to her happiness was her poor health. . . .often during the night she would wake up with a feeling that she was choking. . . .Sitting up, gasping for air, she thought she was going to die. The attacks came more frequently, more severely, and her doctors could do little or nothing for her. She had a form of asthma for which there seemed to be no physical basis. . .medicines offered no relief.

"I knew what it was," she said, "and I knew I would either die or go insane if I couldn't do something about my hatred for my father. . . .That's what was choking me to death!"

It was painful for Belinda to look back on that early time in her life, but with God's help, she did. "Jesus—*you* forgive my father, and then show me how," she prayed.

Something happened as she began to remember. . . .She saw her father, not as a scorned and hated person, but as a man with burdens he was unable to carry—the death of his mother when he was a very little boy. . .years of neglect as the youngest child in a large family whose members had no time to love him. . .the hope for joy in his own wife and children, and the sudden crushing of that hope with the loss of a job. . .the deprivation of unemployment over a long period of time, and the blow to his self-esteem when his wife became the family breadwinner. . .the degradation and self-contempt that must have been his when he turned, in desperation, to what he felt was the one source of happiness in those lonely days—his daughter. . .and the continued confirmation of his worthlessness by his repeated abuse of her. . . .

None of these memories changed the facts for Belinda. The events in her life were the same as she remembered them—except that she no longer hated the pitiful, despairing man her father had become. She understood him, she forgave him, even though she could not alter what he had done—and that understanding saved her life and her sanity. The terrible nighttime attacks of choking began to subside and finally stopped. . . Belinda slept peacefully.

Colleen Townsend Evans

Some time ago a man and his wife came to see me. He had done her a terrible wrong. The wife told me the story and asked what she should do. I said, "I think you ought to shoot him. Have you got a gun?" The husband turned a little pale and said, "She's got two guns."

But then I told her that anybody can return evil for evil, get mad, and fly off the handle. Anybody can feel hurt, pout, carry a grudge, and spoil his own life. But some people have what it takes to rise above some things and become magnificent people.

We talked for a while about the forgiveness of God and the forgiveness of each other. She felt that she could not forgive, but she promised to try. We had a prayer together and they left.

Later, when they came back, they did not need to tell me. I could see in their faces that something wonderful had happened. She said, "It is a miracle, but I have been able to forgive." I stood in the door and watched them leave, knowing that she had become a magnificent person. And he, too, because it takes about as much grace to receive forgiveness as it does to forgive.

The most expensive thing you can do is hold a wrong spirit in your heart against another. The price you pay is the loss, the eternal loss, of your own soul.

Charles L. Allen

But sometimes—no.

It is, however, unquestionable that there are many whose spirits are so locked in behind impenetrable armor that even the greatest efforts to nurture the growth of those spirits are doomed to almost certain failure. To attempt to love someone who cannot benefit from your love with spiritual growth is to waste your energy, to cast your seed upon arid ground. Genuine love is precious, and those who are capable of genuine love know that their loving must be focused as productively as possible through self-discipline.

M. Scott Peck

When you find yourself saying, "Would I do that to you?" or any similar sentence, change it to, "You are different from me, although I find that hard to accept right now." This will open, rather than close, communication between you and the other person.

Begin to view your emotional life as independent of whatever anyone else does. This will free you from the chains of being hurt when others behave differently from the way you want them to.

Wayne W. Dyer

We are not asked to be hurt and hurt again. We are asked to love—and we may have to do that from a distance.

Let then our first act every morning be to make the following resolve for the day: I shall not fear anyone on earth. I shall fear only God. I shall not bear ill will toward anyone. I shall not submit to injustice from anyone. I shall conquer untruth by truth. And in resisting untruth I shall put up with all suffering.

Gandhi

Prayer for the Reader

Dear Saviour, I feel as if my love has been crucified by this betrayal. If that is so, then let that love also be resurrected, in a form more like Yours.

WHEN A CHILD IS IN TROUBLE

"Let your eyes look on the things that are upright."

(Psalm 17:2, NKJV)

At first you can't believe it. Not *your* child! You *know* your child would never do something like that!

Then, when you can no longer deny the evidence, you begin to blame yourself for what went wrong. The accusations pile up: You didn't love your child enough. You loved your child too much. You were too easy; too soft. It's all your fault. If only you had—or hadn't. . . .

Stop right there. Do you see what is happening? While you are blaming yourself, your child is the one who needs your attention.

Oh God, dear God who created him in the first place, please help my blind, naive, misguided child.

"I will go my own way," he says, "I will do my own thing. It's my body and my mind."

He's trying to find himself through sheer physical sensation. He's trying drugs to "expand his mind."

And I am sick with fear. My flesh goes rotten at the thought, my blood is water in my veins.

I am so staggered before this evidence and these words that I don't know where to turn.

Show me, please. Don't let me make a misstep, do something that would turn him against me forever or further damage his life.

Help me, help me, please.

But first—help *him*.

Let your mighty wisdom rouse his own intelligence before it's too late. Make him see that any artificial means toward self-discovery leads to the opposite of what he's seeking.

It is not self-assertion. It is submission to an unknown force beyond his self-control.

It is self-annihilation. It is self-*denial*.

Oh, God, please rescue my child from his self-destruction. Please make him realize its futility and its danger, and help him. Help him now.

Marjorie Holmes

No, your child isn't perfect, not any more than you are. Or anyone else. And this may come as a shock to you. But now you have to face a question: *How* do you love your child? Can you reach out to this flawed, guilt-stricken, frightened young person? Or has your outrage, your shame and your disappointment wiped out that ability? Because at this moment your child needs tangible expressions of your love more than ever before. Not the easy love that springs up from pride in a well-behaved son or daughter. Not the comfortable love that purrs somewhat smugly when you hear about other children getting into trouble. No. This is a hard-to-come-by kind of love that may bring a bitter taste to your mouth. It is nails-piercing-hands love. It isn't earned by a child's perfection, nor is it deserved by obedience. You have to look past the faults to love now, and if you succeed, then you can't even take credit for it. Not really. Because this is the love God has given to you, and it's your turn to pass it on. Oh, yes—when we talk about loving others as Jesus loves us, that includes our own children.

Often I have been asked what Christian love is or what the love of God is all about. The best response I can make to questions like these is to simply suggest that the inquirer take a look at Jesus Christ. That's the place to look because he *is* that love.

Earl F. Palmer

I couldn't remain quiet any longer. I ran to the kitchen, where my mother was preparing our dinner. In tears I told her I had to talk to her, and after one look at my face she dropped everything and took me to her room. Immediately I began confessing to a myriad of petty thefts and lies. Then I proceeded to tell her my greater sins: pounding the next-door neighbor's son, cutting the wiring in a new house with a pair of my father's wire cutters—the list went on, and as I confessed, the need to confess grew. It wasn't long before my father joined us. My parents listened in amazement as their youngest son revealed his life's secret wrongs. I was beside myself attempting to remember all the incidents I might have forgotten and wanted to get out of me. I was desperately looking for a way to release the guilt that had just exploded within me. My mother provided the key. She began telling me a story I had heard many times before but never really understood.

"Jamie, I want you to calm down and listen very carefully to me. I have a story to tell you that will make you feel better about the bad things you did. Now, Jamie, try to listen—Louie, give him a tissue to blow his nose with. . . ."

Dad interjected: "Son, please try to listen to your mother. Here—take this and wipe your eyes. Now look at her while she talks to you. It's all right, even big boys cry sometimes—of course, it doesn't mean you're a sissy. Son, try to—Jamie, listen. That's better. Go ahead, Coke."

"Jamie, you know how much we love you, right? Well, there's Someone Else who loves you more than we ever could—do you know who that is? That's right, Jesus."

It was on that evening that my parents explained to me how Jesus died to take my guilt away from me. He didn't want His friends to feel anxious and guilty about the wrongs they had done. He wanted them to have an abundant life. All I had to do was confess what I had done wrong, and Jesus would lock it up far away where no one would ever see it again. I had heard those words a thousand times before, yet on that night they made sense to me for the first time.

. . . Each time the pain of guilt and anxiety would surface, and I saw myself as a dummy and a bad boy, I would tell myself that Jesus had promised to make me clean and good. Perhaps it was simplistic, but it worked—with consistency.

...Whenever the feelings of guilt returned, telling me I was bad, my Friend wrestled with them. He took on what I was incapable of fighting: my poor self-esteem.

James S. Evans

For many years in my early life I was one of those model children who never gave her parents a moment's worry. Frankly, I think both they and I were blessed with an amazing amount of good fortune. But then one afternoon my girl friend and I went roller skating in front of a school a few blocks away, and neither one of us was aware that this was something we weren't supposed to do. There were no signs to that effect. We were having a marvelous time on the smooth broad strip of concrete when suddenly the school door flew open and a custodian roared out. We stood trembling on our ball bearings while he announced to us that no one was allowed to play on school property after regular school hours and he was going to report us to the principal the very next morning. I'll never forget the shame I felt when he took our names and I tried to imagine what my mother and stepfather would say when they learned that I was *a bad girl*.

I couldn't bring myself to tell them at first. But my parents soon realized that something was wrong because I was just too quiet all evening. Finally they got it out of me. I would be given "a white slip," which was an official reprimand. My transgression would be entered on my otherwise spotless school record—for all time.

My mother was not a patient woman and I expected her to react in anger, which she did, but her anger wasn't directed at me. She was indignant at the unfairness of the penalty. If I had known I was breaking a rule, that would be another matter, she said. But there was no way my girlfriend and I could have known.

The next morning my mother was waiting outside the principal's office when he arrived—not to defend me, but to protest the fact that rules were not posted. Later, I was called to the principal's office where he told me the white slip would not be issued. My record was secure. My mother, in her usual haste, aimed a kiss at my cheek, missed, and ran to catch her bus to work.

The true servant, however, by definition is not at his or her own disposition, but is at the disposition of others. Servants are those whose plans are always interrupted by the plans of others. The servant is one who cannot stand on rights, not being aware of having any. The servant cannot go off at will or stand aloof, but is always there for the other. To be a servant is to show mercy, to step outside the realm of rights and duties, the world of scorecards and ledger sheets, in order to give to others freely and from the heart.

Luke Timothy Johnson

Well, you can say, I was lucky. I really didn't do anything wrong. But I *felt* as if I had. I *saw* myself as guilty, and later in my life, when I did break some rules, I knew that shattering feeling again. Being wrong, doing something wrong, devastates whatever self-esteem we have. But we can repair the damage as long as we know that some part of us is worth the effort. And that is where parents come in.

How do I explain the shock of finding a heap of beer and liquor bottles in the basement, covered over by an old tarpaulin; the panic that propelled me up the stairs to the children's bedrooms, frantically searching for some clue to understanding what had been going on in my absence; the shame of picking up a diary and opening it, violating their trust, searching for evidence that they had violated mine; my despair at finding it—the documentation of parties in my absence, with the note: *I hope Mom doesn't find out.*

. . . All I know is that I ran to my car and pulled away and was speeding out of town, onto a highway headed north.

I opened the car window to dry tears that wouldn't stop and I was hollering at the wind: "How could they do that to me? How could they betray me? They know how hard I'm working. I tried to be understanding of them. 'Why?' As I pictured the clandestine parties in *our house*...the booze...drugs...I became so nauseated, I had to pull off the road. I rested my head on the steering wheel.

I must have slept, for the sun was near setting when I straightened up and looked about. I didn't know where I was. Some lights of a distant village were coming on and I drove toward them.

At a crossroads was a darkened church...I got out of the car and sat on its steps....

On the one hand, they had broken a trust I had placed in them. They had let me down. And on the other hand, I was terribly ashamed that I had violated my own cardinal rule of privacy, the sanctity of a diary.

...The long drive back gave me plenty of time to think. Perhaps as I'd been focusing on my own need to grow, shoring up my own confidence in the world of work, I'd been ducking the additional job of being a leader to my children. I'd been counting on love and understanding to see us through. When it wasn't there, I'd bolted.

They were seated on the sofa. A mass of spaghetti was congealed in a pot on the stove. The table was set. No one had eaten.

"Where have you been?" Billy asked.

Looking at the three of them—Ann and Shawn, with their swollen eyes and blotchy cheeks, Billy, stern and pale—I could only whisper, "I left you." And Shawn shuddered. "You can't do that. What would we do without you?" And I said: "I came back. I'm your mother." And then we were all crying and I said that we'd broken each other's trust and that we had to start from scratch but we could do it.

I took a deep breath and said: "This is our home. And we are going to have rules to protect it. And you are my children and I am going to fight tooth and nail to protect you. If you don't like it, that's tough. I'm your mother and I'm not going to give up. Ever. I love you too much. Now then."

I got a yellow pad and we all sat around the dining room table. At the top of the pad I wrote: *Our Family Covenant.* Then we discussed those things we valued that made our home precious to us, and what it was we felt we had a right to expect of each other. And I wrote:

Because we are a family and because we want to live together in this house, we agree:

1. No parties without Mom's O.K.

2. We don't want people on drugs in our house.

3. Drunk grown-ups aren't welcome either.

...We signed the paper and I taped it to the refrigerator door. It stayed there for several weeks although we never had to refer to it again....

Parenting, I found out, is more than caring and comforting. It's also teaching and leading. Billy said later: "We were waiting for you to take charge. We're proud of you. And we're proud of our family, too."

Thank God, they waited for me.

Marilyn Jensen

I have always marveled at parents who stand by children who have committed a terrible crime. How could they condone such things? I asked myself. But now I realize that by loving their children parents are not excusing their sins. They are not closing their eyes to them any more than Christ overlooked our sins, the ones that put Him on the cross. In their times of trial, parents may discover what love really is.

The first thing that love must do is communicate these three things: I truly care about you. I really want your happiness and I will do all I can to assure it. You are a uniquely valuable person.

John Powell

Love doesn't puff itself up, Paul tells us, and that may be the most difficult thing a parent has to learn. Love doesn't beat its chest and brag about the good child—when the child is good. No. Sometimes love has to sift through the ashes of a child's rubbled life and find something, however small, worth building on.

Peter and I were at the Eighth Precinct station from 3:30 until 6:30. . . . I was impressed with the way the District of Columbia handled these first offenders. Each boy, with his parents, had to appear before a judge. As I remember it, these were private sessions. When Peter and I appeared before a kindly judge for our talk, to my surprise the judge raised the issue I had considered too prideful. "Peter, your father stood for something in the greater Washington community. You have a proud heritage. Don't tarnish it. Son, I want you to think deeply about all this."

In the aftermath of this episode, I saw that the wall between young Peter and me was in part my doing. The wall remained because I had failed to share with Peter at the depth of spirit. Our whole relationship had been pitched too much on the level of daily schedules, material things—all the superficialities of life between a mother and her 16-year-old son.

Was it too late to change this? I would try. The inner Voice instructed me to open the depths of my own life and feelings to Peter and share with him. How much he would understand, I could not know. My business was to *obey*. God would have to take care of the rest.

Catherine Marshall

I used to play baseball, and my father went to the games because he was always interested in whatever his children did. I remember one game especially. It was a tight game, and I happened to get a long hit. I was running around the bases as fast as I could, but I seemed to gain added strength when I heard him shouting above the crowd, "Come on home, Charles, come on home." Since he has been gone, there have been times when the going was a little harder for me and I have been tempted to do less than my best, but then I could hear him saying, "Come on home, Charles, come on home."

Charles L. Allen

Prayer for the Reader

How many times, Jesus, have I asked You to be patient with me, to love me in spite of my mistakes? And now my child needs as much from me and may not be able to ask for it. Is my disappointment drowning out his cries for help? Is my own shame preventing him from speaking? I don't want that to happen, Lord. I don't care if I have to shout out loud—I want my child to know how much I love him. Give me Your voice.

WHEN SOMEONE YOU LOVE IS SUDDENLY KILLED

"Then the king was deeply moved, and went up to the chamber over the gate and wept..."O Absalom my son, my son!"

(II Samuel 18:33, NKJV)

I knew, the moment I drove down my street, that something was wrong. There were too many cars parked along the curb, and most of them I didn't recognize. Every light in the house next to mine was lit, but there were no sounds of a party. As I pulled into my driveway I wondered if I should ring the Hales' bell and find out what was going on. Then I decided I wouldn't. Something in me didn't want to know.

But I had no choice. The Hales' door opened and I saw Jenny. The expression on her face frightened me. I had never seen such pain.

"Harry's dead!" she said in a whisper that sliced across the lawn.

It made no sense. Harry, the Hales' oldest son, wasn't quite thirty. He was in good health. How could he be dead?

I got out of my car as Jenny came toward me. "He was shot," she said, and her eyes told me that she still couldn't believe it. "Right in front of his apartment. A man walked up to him and shot him and took his watch. Harry's dead!"

I have read of such things. We all have. But it's different when it happens to someone you know. It's suddenly real. And frightening.

"My child is dead," Jenny whimpered. I put my arms around her thin shoulders and held her close, both of us crying. I wanted to say something that would help, but no words came to my mind. Only anger and hatred and a fierce desire for vengeance.

I knew that was wrong. I'm a Christian and I didn't think a Christian should ever feel that way. A Christian should find words of comfort. But where? How? A Christian should do something. What? What can anyone do? Except weep?

It was a long, strange evening for all of us. The Hales' house was filled with friends and family, and none of us knew what to do, what to say. We were choking on our anger, our bitterness, our fear, and feeling guilty because what we really wanted to do was shout out loud at God. But that

229

didn't seem to be the proper way to address God, so we all kept silent. And distant. From each other and from God. We didn't think God would understand what we were going through.

> So—you feel like screaming, not just crying. Find a place and do so! Wise counselors are needed for you and each one of your family. Do not leave the festering pain as is. Go to the counselor of your choice. Yes, you are strong enough to bear it alone. It will take longer.
>
> *Wayne E. Oates*

Later, as I lay in the darkness, trying to sleep and not succeeding, I wondered about that assumption of ours. Why *wouldn't* God understand? He knew what violence was. He understood hatred, fear, rage. He saw what they did to His world, and it was into that very world He sent His Son. Jesus walked our streets and felt our fears, and He did it as a human being. He understood, all right. He still does. Yes, we can come to Him in anger, in confusion, or in any of our human ways. Because He will understand.

We can ask Him those questions that torment us: *Why? Why this one I loved? Why someone innocent?* We can beat our fists against His chest and demand a reason for our heartbreak—and His own tears will spill over onto our upturned faces. Yes, He understands. He receives our pain, and weeps—as surely as He wept when John the Baptist was killed. He was there. He knows.

But, no, He will not give you answers to your questions, because none will suffice. Tell me, honestly, is there any answer that will make a difference in your loss? Are there any words that will dry your tears, let you sleep at night, cease your dread of beginning another day without the one you love? Of course not. And that is something you must accept.

> The problem of pain, of war and the horror of war, of poverty and disease is always confronting us. But a God who allows no

pain, no grief, also allows no choice. There is little unfairness in a colony of ants, but there is also little freedom. We human beings have been given the terrible gift of free will, and this ability to make choices, to help write our own story, is what makes us human, even when we make the wrong choices, abusing our freedom and the freedom of others. The weary and war-torn world around us bears witness to the wrongness of many of our choices. But lest I stumble into despair I remember, too, seeing the white, pinched-faced little children coming to the pediatric floor of a city hospital for open-heart surgery, and seeing them, two days later, with colour in their cheeks, while the nurses tried to slow down their wheel-chair races. I remember, too, that there is now a preventive for trachoma, still the chief cause of blindness in the world. And I remember that today few mothers die in childbirth, and our graveyards no longer contain the mute witness of five little stones in a row, five children of one family, dead in a week of scarlet fever or diphtheria.

Madeleine L'Engle

There is no replacement for the one you have lost. None. But neither is there vengeance. Turning away from the world will only aggravate the pain and keep you close to it. Resenting the happiness of others who still have their loved ones with them will only keep the death news vibrant, throbbing. You need healing. And there is only one Physician. Let Him care for you.

Recently I went to Washington, D.C., on business. But there was something more important I wanted to do there. I took a cab to the Mall and walked along the highly polished black-granite Vietnam Veterans Memorial. It was beautiful and hauntingly dramatic, a fitting tribute to the 57,939 names of the fallen engraved on it.

A park ranger turned the pages in a huge book. His finger sought it out. "Panel 15E," he said quietly. "Line 38."

I walked down the pathway until I found Panel 15E and counted down the lines etched into the gleaming, reflecting granite. There it was: Channing Allen, Jr. I stared at it, trying to bring my feelings into focus. But all I could see through my misting eyes was a freckled-faced 12-year-old on a Little League mound, grinning down at the batter.

I had been Chippy's manager; he was my star pitcher and we understood each other perfectly. I, the cautious disciplinarian, the man "in charge." Chippy, the sometimes serious, often rollicking, fun-loving man-child growing into a great future. I'd cherished him from the start of our relationship....

It was years ago that I'd heard how he'd been killed by a sniper's bullet in Vietnam while helping evacuate his comrades who had been wounded. The news had ruined my desire to see any more Little League games.

I reached up and ran my fingers over Chippy's name. Then I strode quickly away. But I had noted other names as I sought his. Chippy was in a well-mixed lineup. John Hornyak . . . Ismael Soto . . . Carmine Genovese . . . Leonard Gurwitz . . . Tyrone Jackson . . . Peter Schmidt. A lineup as varied as our own Tiger team; Kelley . . . DiMassio . . . Rappoport . . . Stankowicz. Both sets of names were in perfect American counterpoint. And I knew I could no longer repudiate all that Chippy Allen had epitomized. Not to watch kids play ball again was a false estrangement from reality and unworthy of that name in black granite.

This year I was at the opening of the Little League season, enjoying it immensely. And praying that names like Hornyak, Genovese, Gurwitz, Soto—and Allen—would never again be etched in a stone war memorial.

Jerome Brondfield

You will be healed—but there will be a scar. Your life—*you*—will never be the same. How could you be? Someone who was part of you is gone. But you can go on. And you can give to others what you gave before. Even more. You can give in behalf of the person you lost—just as Jesus gave in behalf of John. You can live, here on earth, for that other and for yourself. God will help you. He is here.

Prayer for the Reader

I am empty, Father. I am bitter, even toward You. I grieve, not only for the one I have lost, but for the loving part of myself that seems to have died as well. You, Who have at other times brought the dead back to life, revive my dead ability to love, to be close, to care about this world and those I know. I believe, I insist, that You can heal this mortal wound.

WHEN THE TRUTH MIGHT HURT SOMEONE

*"Create in me a clean heart, O God;
and renew a right spirit within me."*

(Psalm 51:100, KJV)

You'd rather not say anything. You might be misunderstood. But you know you must speak up. If you don't, you won't be able to live with yourself—or with God.

Wouldn't it be nice if love could always speak sweet words and high praise? Sometimes it can. But not now.

> This man is so difficult to work with, God. So difficult I think sometimes I can't stand it.
>
> Everything about him annoys me, upsets and repels me. And he must sense this, because whatever I do, I find him impossible to please.
>
> God, we will never get any place until I overcome this feeling of active and intense dislike. So bless him.
>
> *Marjorie Holmes*

You will need courage. By acting in love you will risk losing the one you love. This is one of those times you love the person, but not what the person is doing. Eventually your friend will be hurt—and *that* is your concern.

> . . .When I was very young and overzealous to the point of arrogance, I wanted so much for others to have the spiritual experience I felt I had, that I encountered everyone on everything I thought was wrong. I spoke the truth—and nothing else; there was no love in what I said. The results were disastrous. I was president of our church college department at the time, and suddenly executive board members began quitting right and left.
>
> . . .One day a man I knew well, the advisor to the college department, sat me down and had a talk with me. Because I

knew he loved me, I could accept the truth from him. He was firm, yet kind, as he told me that the way to stimulate enthusiasm was not to make heavy demands on people and then write them cutting letters when they fell short of them—which I had done. This, he explained, was why everyone was quitting.

I had been completely unaware of what I had been doing. . . . The truth hurt, but because this man had offered it to me in an attitude of love, I saw I had done wrong. I felt ashamed, but not rejected. . . . He knew how much of the truth I could handle, and not once did he allow himself to use a word or an expression that would have put me down. . . . his faith in me gave me the confidence to look for more loving ways to communicate my hopes and dreams.

Louis H. Evans, Jr.

. . .True love should. . .invite the beloved to "stretch," to grow beyond the old limitations, to attempt what was always considered too difficult, to break a self-destructive habit that has always been too overpowering, to rise above a fear, to give up a grudge, to open a repressed feeling, to confront a difficult situation, to offer a painful apology.

John Powell

Face it—you may get hurt. You may lose a friend or someone else who means a great deal to you. But you will not lose your ability to love, and that is what the issue is all about.

Prayer for the Reader

I must think carefully, lovingly, Lord, before I speak. I wish I knew softer words to wrap around hard realities. But even if I stammer, or if the thoughts come rushing out in less than gentle ways, let my love go with them. Let my devotion be louder than my voice.

HOW MUCH CAN I AFFORD TO GIVE?

"Give as freely as you have received."

(Matthew 10:8, Living Bible)

How much? Everything.
What you own. What you are. There can be no holding back.

> Those who want nothing from the world of men and things and yet are willing to share everything, because they feel so deeply, are the meek. . . .They are terrible in that they want nothing, and hence cannot be tempted or bought, and in that they are willing to go to any lengths for others because they feel so deeply. Christ standing before Pilate is a picture of the Terrible Meek. He could not be bought or bullied, for He wanted nothing—nothing except to give His life for the very men who were crucifying him.
>
> *E. Stanley Jones*

We are very investment-conscious these days. We count our dividends, compute interest rates and look for the best return on what we are willing to invest. Someday it will all come back to us!

> When we pray for our daily bread and our heavenly Father provides the loaf, we must remember that it is not ours alone. It must be divided—because there are those who do not know how to ask and those who do ask and whom God intends to answer through us. Some will receive their life resources only through our stewardship. Our daily bread then becomes the means to do what God wants us to do in this world.
>
> *Colleen Townsend Evans*

We are God's dividends. He has invested His love in us. He has given us His Son, at great cost to Him. But instead of giving back to Him all that we are and all that we have, we are to give it to our brothers and sisters. We have the honor to be our Father's servants.

But we are easily influenced by our world and its values. We think of giving strictly in terms of money. Giving is more than that. It is not keeping track of what is given or how much is left over. It is not figuring out what percentage belongs to God and how much we can keep for ourselves. It is, frankly, not caring about such things, but rather counting on God's ability to provide us with enough to give more. That requires more courage than I usually can muster.

When a surplus comes my way, I am very generous, and I must say I enjoy the feeling. But let my bank account go down to a few lonely figures and I look with suspicion on the outstretched hand.

And yet the most giving person I have known is a woman who is truly poor. Joann McCoy cannot work because she is losing her eyesight. She suffers from an illness that keeps her confined: she has agoraphobia, a severe form of anxiety attack that literally keep her a prisoner in the familiar surroundings of her home. Her telephone is her lifeline to the world, and she uses it to serve God in the only way she can. She runs a counseling hot line for others who suffer from agoraphobia and cannot get out for the help they need. When they are desperate, Joann urges them to hang onto their faith so that they will be cured. She finds the words and prayers to calm them when they are near hysteria.

Every penny Joann McCoy has goes to the telephone company, and many times her phone service has been temporarily disconnected until she gets the money to pay her bills. I have talked to her when she was using a neighbor's phone to continue her work, and sometimes she had no more than five dollars between her and destitution. But she keeps on giving. And somehow God keeps on providing. Joann counts on that. She even gives her faith to others.

Prayer for the Reader

Help me to let go of my blessings, Jesus—or I will surely lose them.

KEEPING THY BROTHER

"And this commandment have we from him, That he who loveth God love his brother also."

(I John 4:21, KJV)

Kevin looked around the big old house my husband and I had just bought and all he saw was the space in it. "Gee, don't you feel guilty living here, just the two of you?" he asked. "You should take in a couple of refugees." He wasn't joking. He was serious. He was still in school; he had never known money problems. The fact that we had to earn the money to fix up an old house and make it livable didn't impress him.

"You could camp out here," he said, as if he thought that would be a wonderful lifestyle. Later, out of school and both a husband and a father, Kevin would change his mind. He would still be generous, but he would realize that a line has to be drawn—somewhere.

But—where? Where do we begin, and where do we end, the keeping of a brother? It was a brother-in-law who helped me find the answer. Or perhaps part of it.

Chris was younger than Kevin by a few years. He had always had trouble in school and still couldn't read well. Teachers kept passing him on to someone else and finally he graduated from high school. But he could go no farther—and to him that was a relief. School had been an agony. Life was an agony. The only alternative for Chris was—drugs. He was "into" them, deeply. Not the "heavy stuff," as they call it. But given time, he would get there.

Chris needed a change of scene, his mother thought, and we agreed. We brought him to live with us—in the big old house we were fixing up. In a sense, we had our refugee.

And we loved him dearly. It was hard not to. Don't let the drugs prejudice you—Chris is one of the sweetest-natured persons I have ever known. He was too troubled to do much about anything that bothered you, but he sure knew when you had a problem. And he felt it with you.

My husband and I didn't know how to handle him. Should we mention the pot smoking? Should we look for signs that he was still doing it, even though we had laid down the law before he moved in? What should we do if we found incriminating evidence? I remember praying for Chris often during those days, but I really didn't know what to pray for. I wondered how much experience God had had with a drug habit.

For a while we fooled ourselves into believing that Chris was walking the straight and narrow. He was benefiting from his new environment. We were good for him. How nice!

And how horrible it was to come home one day and find him dazed on the living-room sofa, all six-feet-two of him lying like a bag of bones and a silly grin on his face.

It was the grin that got to me. I went into a rage.

"Get up!" I shouted.

He blinked. The smile froze. I had never raised my voice to him.

"*Up!*" I commanded.

He couldn't pull himself together, but he tried. That was all I needed. I seized a handful of his thick, dark hair and pulled him almost upright, forcing him to look at me.

"This is *my* home!" I said, two inches away from him. "I will not allow you to destroy yourself in it. I will not allow you to use drugs in it. If you want to stay here, understand that we want you. But you will have to follow *our* rules!"

He wasn't smiling. He began to cry.

"Don't you *dare* cry!" I said, determined not to let him get to me. Besides, I was too angry to feel sorry for him. We had had enough of pity.

In that one moment I realized that keeping a brother is something we must do. Always. But in what way? Keeping is not the giving of material things, or understanding, or tears, although there will be times when they are needed—but only as expressions of a Jesus-kind of caring that makes them possible. We can keep a brother only if we accept a loving responsibility for him. Keeping means protecting and nurturing a God-created part of a person—not giving him the means or the permission to destroy himself.

Love is not simply giving; it is *judicious* giving and judicious withholding as well. It is judicious praising and judicious crit-

239

icizing. It is judicious arguing, struggling, confronting, urging, pushing and pulling in addition to comforting. It is leadership. The word *judicious* means requiring judgment, and judgment requires more than instinct; it requires thoughtful and often painful decision-making.

M. Scott Peck

"Give to him that asketh"—not necessarily what he asks, but be so full that you will give him something, perhaps more than he asks—and better. His real need may be money—then give it to him, not necessarily *all* that he asks, for that might conflict with the legitimate askings of one's own family, but give to him. He may ask you for money, and you may see that merely to give him money is a cheap and easy and ruinous way out. You must give him more—you must give him the disposition, if possible, to stand on his own feet and be self-respecting.

E. Stanley Jones

We are keepers, not rulers, and we must be careful not to intrude on God's domain. We cannot decide what a brother is meant to be. We only know that he is intended to be worthwhile. If a line must be drawn, then we must ask God to draw it for us. And we must not cross it—even if it means loving from the other side.

Chris did try to follow our rules. He didn't succeed. Or so we thought when he decided to go back to live with his mother. But something had happened to him while he was with us. That was a few years ago. He has a job now; not anything spectacular, but his boss says he is the most dependable worker he has ever hired. Chris keeps to himself on his own time. His sister is trying to teach him to read. He can, a little, but it's a struggle. We think he isn't using drugs, but we're not sure. Chris seems to know that people love him. That they care about what happens to him. And that they strongly disapprove of the fact that he doesn't care much about himself.

I think Chris realizes that he *is* a brother, and that love keeps.

Prayer for the Reader

Make demands on me, Lord. Make me face up to my lack of patience, my shortness of temper when someone needs more than I have to give. Do the giving through me. Don't allow me to turn away from someone who needs my love. Force my heart open, even if it hurts, and let me be the means of bringing You into an empty life.

HOW MANY TIMES SHOULD I FORGIVE?

"Be kind to one another; be understanding. Be as ready to forgive others as God for Christ's sake has forgiven you."

(Ephesians 4:32, Phillips)

Would seven times be enough to forgive someone? Peter asked, no doubt supposing he was the greatest forgiver of all time.

No, that would not be sufficient, replied Jesus. Seventy times seven would be better. And of course what He meant is that we should forgive. Period. Always. Period.

Jesus wasn't asking us to do the impossible, only what is excruciatingly hard.

If we forgive positively, we'll take the initiative in forgiving. I have great difficulty here. If someone apologizes, then I'm usually willing to bury the hatchet, but it's tougher when I've been wronged (or think I have) and my enemy doesn't even admit his error.

What about the obnoxious fellow who never says "I'm sorry"? Here we can profit by noticing how it is that Christ forgives us. The startling thing about divine love is that God did not wait until we had apologized to send his Son. He took the initiative. He took the first step.

. . .When you have been loved in such a fashion, you want to change. Think for a moment about the people who have influenced you for good, who have brought out the best in you. Aren't they the people who have taken the initiative with you, who have believed in you, and forgiven your faults? And because they accepted you as you were, you wanted to change.

Alan Loy McGinnis

A few years ago I was deeply hurt by a friend who didn't even seem to realize she had done something wrong. And by wrong I mean something dishonest which cost me dearly. It took me a long time to get back on my feet financially, but then I had a more staggering problem confronting me. I couldn't forgive the woman. It was no use trying to talk to God about it—there was too much hatred in my heart. And I didn't want to let it go.

> Those who bear the Cross must also bear others' burdens. This includes the burden of responsibility for sin as well as the sharing of suffering. What room can there possibly be for touchiness or a self-regarding fastidiousness in the true burden-bearer? Forgiveness is a clear-eyed and coolheaded acceptance of the burden of responsibility.
>
> *Elisabeth Elliot*

A few years passed and my hatred remained, like a lump stuck in my soul. It bothered me. I began asking God to help me to get rid of it. Maybe then I could forgive.

Not long ago my friend called me up—out of the blue. Maybe something was bothering her, too. I'll never know. But all my bitterness began to dissolve as we talked. We didn't even touch on the matter that destroyed our relationship—because I realized that she still isn't aware of it. I also came face to face with the fact that it is my responsibility to look out for my own interests. I can't delegate that to anyone except myself and God.

My discovery may seem small to you, but it was monumental to me. It gave me freedom by alerting me to the real source of my hatred: me. I had been furious at myself for allowing someone to make a fool of me, but it was easier for me to blame my foolish friend than to blame myself. Once I could accept my own mistakes—and forgive them—I could stop hating my friend.

I'm not sure about this, but perhaps hating often begins with ourselves. Perhaps forgiveness has to begin there, too. What I am sure about is that God is the One Who cleared the way to forgiveness for me. I never could have got there by myself.

And now that I think about it, out of all the times I prayed for the power to forgive, the prayer I remember most clearly is this:

Prayer for the Reader

Help me, Lord Jesus. I still can't forgive her. I'm still hating her. I have tried. I have prayed. I think I just don't have enough love in me. I've never asked You this before, but will You forgive for me? Will You do what I can't?

TURNING THE OTHER CHEEK

"...I cried unto thee, and thou hast healed me."

(Psalm 30:2, KJV)

They tried to stop Him from loving them. They couldn't.

They insulted Him. They ridiculed His manner of speech, His clothing. They criticized the company He kept.

They invited Him to their homes out of curiosity. He was a conversation piece to some of them. Most of the time He slept under the stars.

They threatened Him. A few of them even tried to change His mind because they could see what was going to happen to Him.

They betrayed Him. Lied to Him. Arrested Him. Told Him that if only He would stop loving them, He could go free.

They spat at Him. Beat Him mercilessly. Humiliated Him in the streets leading to the cross. And there they thought they had ended it—Him and all His loving.

And they failed.

And there is nothing anyone can do to make *you* stop loving. So, yes, you can turn your other cheek. As many times as you must.

One does not have to understand to be obedient. Instead of understanding—that intellectual understanding which we are so fond of—there is a feeling of rightness, of knowing, knowing things which we are not yet able to understand....

As long as we know what it's about, then we can have the courage to go wherever we are asked to go, even if we fear that the road may take us through danger and pain.

Madeleine L'Engle

...We must not be surprised if we are in for a rough time. When a man turns to Christ and seems to be getting on pretty well (in the sense that some of his bad habits are now corrected), he often feels that it would now be natural if things went fairly smoothly. When troubles come along—illnesses, money troubles, new kinds of temptations—he is disappointed. These things, he feels, might have been necessary to rouse him and make him repent in his bad old days; but why now? Because God is forcing him on, or up, to a higher level: putting him into situations where he will have to be very much braver, or more patient, or more loving, than he ever dreamed of being before. It seems to us all unnecessary: but that is because we have not yet had the slightest notion of the tremendous thing He means to make of us.

C. S. Lewis

Prayer for the Reader

Heal me with Your love, O my Lord. And then let me love again.

3

THE EVERYDAY DISCIPLE—

THOU SHALT
AND
THOU SHALT NOT

Either you follow Him. Or you don't.

And if you do, then you follow Him all the time. There is no such thing as a part-time disciple.

You follow Him wherever He goes, even to the cross. You go on with Him from there.

You go wherever He sends you. You will not always be welcome. He has prepared you for hostility, for opposition. You will not be overcome by it, not if you let Him sustain you.

He will ask you to do many things you cannot do. Or so you think. But He knows you better than you know yourself. You will learn a lot about yourself—*if* you follow Him every day, every moment. You can't commit in some things and not in others. You can't make up your own rules. You must obey Him.

But the way of a disciple is not grim. If anything, it is glorious, because Christ has also prepared you for love. Let me tell you a few of the things He will enable you to do.

You will know yourself. You will not be trying to please the world, only

God. And He loves what you truly are. In fact, He will lead you into a discovery of your innermost needs and teach you how to fulfill them. You will like the person you are.

You will experience much deeper, more gratifying relationships with others. You will lose your fear of getting close to people. You will not hesitate to ask for what you need, to give what is needed. You will always receive, but not always from others. God will see to it that you are well cared for. You will never be without Him.

You will change things in this world. Perhaps not a lot. But you will leave your mark on it. Life here will be better, not only for you, but for those who come after you go on.

And you will go on. The life of a disciple does not end. You are already living in eternity if you are serving Jesus Christ today.

This book was created by the same staff that prepares *Guideposts*, a monthly magazine filled with true stories of people's adventures in faith.

If you have found inspiration in *Coping*, we think you'll find monthly help and inspiration in the exciting stories that appear in our magazine.

Guideposts is not sold on the newsstand. It's available by subscription only. And subscribing is easy. All you have to do is write Guideposts Associates, Inc., Carmel, New York 10512. A year's subscription costs only $5.95 in the United States, $7.95 in Canada and overseas.

When you subscribe, each month you can count on receiving exciting new evidence of God's presence and bountiful expressions of His unlimited love and care for each one of us.